Mastering
the Internet

Ian Shircore and Richard Lander

Orion Business Toolkit

ORION
BUSINESS
BOOKS

For my children, Zoë and Nicholas
Ian Shircore

For Sarah, Rebecca and Benjamin who make the world go round
Richard Lander

Copyright © 1999 by Ian Shircore and Richard Lander

All rights reserved

The right of Ian Shircore and Richard Lander to be identified
as the authors of this work has been asserted by them in accordance
with the Copyright, Designs and Patents Act 1988

First published in Great Britain in 1998 by
Orion Business

An imprint of The Orion Publishing Group Ltd
Orion House, 5 Upper St Martin's Lane, London WC2H 9EA

A CIP catalogue record for this book
is available from the British Library

ISBN 0–75281–358–7

Typeset by Deltatype Ltd, Birkenhead, Merseyside
Printed and bound in Great Britain by
Clays Ltd, St Ives plc.

Contents

Chapter 1

Where do you want to have been tomorrow?

'We must master our good fortune, or it will master us.'

(Publilius Syrus, 1st c. BC)

➡ IT'S NOT JUST FOR OTHER PEOPLE

One morning, Gregor Samsa woke up and discovered that he was a beetle. Don't you just hate it when that happens?

Each of us starts from the same place, at a different time. One day something changes. Something happens at work or we overhear a chance remark somewhere and we suddenly realise that the Internet is about to become real for us, too. We've always known it was going on out there, for other people. All of a sudden, we realise it is going to touch us as well. And that can feel just like waking up as a beetle.

The hero of Kafka's story, *Metamorphosis*, found that everything in his life was different after this change. Within a few years, the Internet and the World Wide Web will have brought about extraordinary changes in all our lives, though anyone who starts telling you with any confidence what those changes will be is certainly bluffing. We can't know, because the future is always so fuzzy and open-ended and divergent. We look back at the world five years ago and it seems crisp and sharp, like yesterday. We look forward the same distance and we don't know what tax rates will be, who'll be in government or what currency we'll be using. We don't even know if there'll be a world to look forward to. What this book offers – and what makes it different from all the other Internet books on the shelves – is a bit of informed realism. Our aim is to help you get a handle on what you and your business might want to do with the Internet in the next year or two. For absolute beginners, there is enough guidance here to get you started on connecting to the Web, using e-mail and tapping the immense resources of knowledge and information available on the Internet. But there are already lots of 'how-to' books that will take you step by step through all those mechanical routines, as if they were an end in themselves.

This is the 'how-to' book that tackles the bigger questions. How are you going to use the Internet? What can you do – as an entrepreneur, a boss, an executive or even a very junior manager – to introduce or suggest new and better ways of working? How can knowing the current trends and possibilities make a real difference in your work? And if the world is changing so fast, what should you be thinking about doing next Monday morning?

➡ A POINT-AND-CLICK WORLD

It is the Web that is powering the explosive growth of the Internet. It is vivid, visual, colourful, accessible and magnetically attractive, partly because it is the nearest thing we've ever seen to drive-it-yourself television. And it can take you anywhere.

Point and click is the secret. Point and click here and you can search a worldwide database for financial statistics. Point and click there and you can view the build-up of rush-hour traffic as you look down from a camera over a Los Angeles freeway. Point and click to buy a CD at half price half a world away and have it shipped to you at a total cost that's still less than you'd pay in the High Street. Point and click to switch to e-mail and send a message to 20 colleagues in 20 countries for less than the cost of one inland stamp.

Point and click to download free software, NASA's photos from space, a list of hotels in Madrid and all the up-to-the-minute news you can take. Point and click to see a live rock concert or listen to the Test Match commentary. Point and click for information, excitement, surprises, wisdom and inanity – all in huge quantities. Point. And click. And usually, it has to be said, wait.

The secret of this extraordinary richness, power and flexibility is the browser, a software window on the world devised by Marc

Andreessen, then a 22-year-old undergraduate in Illinois, back in 1993. Browsers are easy to use and look engagingly simple, though they are immensely subtle and complex under the skin. They can take you to any of the millions of sites on the World Wide Web and they also give you an all-round Internet launchpad, enabling you to use e-mail and exploit the other resources of the Net.

➡ BEGINNERS FOR 15 MINUTES

When you first set eyes on a browser, loaded on a PC, you see a large window that takes up most of the screen and a smaller open box above it, marked 'Address' or 'Location'. Type the address of a Website into the address panel, press 'return' and you are taken to the opening page, or home page, of the site you requested. When you are looking at a page, notice the tabs, push-buttons, images and bits of differently coloured or underlined text that are the Web designer's way of inviting you to move on to some related page you might be interested in. When one of these links catches your eye, point at it with your cursor and click the left button of your mouse and you will be taken there. It is so brilliantly straightforward. Just point and click – and occasionally type in a new address. Point and click. It's a way of operating a computer that's so easy, even an adult can understand.

Because of the inspired simplicity of this approach, nobody stays a complete beginner for long. The rewards come thick and fast and people seldom need telling twice about how to perform the basic operation of visiting a site on the Web. After 15 minutes, the absolute beginner has already graduated to the well-populated ranks of 'inexperienced users', which is one reason why books about the Internet that claim to be for complete beginners have a very short useful lifespan. With such an intuitive system, the learning is in the doing. People may need to come back and refer to a book to find out how to use the 'Reload/refresh' button to restart a page that has stalled during loading or to check that simply clicking on 'Print' will print out the page they are looking at, but they are basically on their way within a matter of minutes. And even clicking on completely the wrong button isn't going to mean the end of the world. No-one has ever died yet from nudging the wrong command on Microsoft's Internet Explorer or Netscape Navigator, the two browsers that serve more than 95 per cent of the Web's users.

You can make mistakes without hurting your own computer, your browser or any of the distant apparatus of the Internet or the site. There are between 20 and 30 buttons, menu items, icons and panels that appear when you load your browser – yet you can probably get by with no more than eight of them (all right, then: the address panel, the e-mail icon, 'Back' and 'Forward', 'Reload', 'Stop', 'Print' and 'File', to allow you to save material to your hard disk). People can make it all as complicated as they want, but it is because the fundamentals are so sublimely painless that browsers have managed to drag computer communications out of the ghettos of the technically aware and into the mainstream of life and business, where it is about to make its presence felt in some very dramatic and far-reaching ways.

➡ THERE ARE STILL FORTUNES TO BE MADE

For a start, the Internet is going to change the way we work. This book is full of examples of the sort of changes that have already been seen in businesses large and small and the sort of changes – like the introduction of micropayments, allowing you to buy things for perhaps a fifth of a penny – that have yet to materialise.

It is going to open up undreamed-of opportunities to create new businesses and to generate personal wealth, which is one reason why we have included, in Appendix B, our guide to 'Seven Ways to Make a Fortune via the Internet'. These are all perfectly sound, viable ideas that have not yet been exploited in the United Kingdom or most other countries outside the United States. Indeed, some cannot be done at all yet, though they will become quite possible sooner than most people might imagine. Above all, these are not descriptions of how past fortunes have been made, but ideas that could be started here and now, or somewhere nearby and in the very near future.

Do you fancy the idea of publishing your own e-mail newsletter, for example? As long as you can offer something that people will be interested to read, there is nothing to stop you, because the costs involved are so minute, compared with printing and distributing printed paper. If you have access to e-mail, try e-mailing the publishers of this book, Orion, at *businessbooks@orionbooks.co.uk*, for a thought-provoking illustration of how quick, cheap and easy newsletter publishing can be. The software at the publisher's end will automatically note your e-mail address and send you, almost instantly, the latest edition of the Orion Business Books e-mail magazine (or e-zine, if you must), telling you about other leading-edge business titles from Orion.

This will cost you a sum equal to the minimum price of a local phone call, since you will only need to be connected for a few seconds. It will cost Orion much the same, because the newsletter will be downloaded to you well within the minimum call charge time. There are no admin costs, as this whole transaction is untouched by human hand. All that's required is a facility called an autoresponder, or autobot, built into the e-mail software. This is sometimes free, but sometimes costs money, depending on the deal a business has with the company providing its Internet connection. Even if it is charged for, though, the price per autoresponder is usually no more than £3 to £5 a month, which is

Honor you TROPHY catch or your child's FIRST BASS or TROUT with our THANK-U THANK-U commorative plaque. Each 8" X 10" wood and brass plaque is custom engraved with all of the pertinent information regarding that memorable day. Location, date, species, weight & length along with the angler's name, age/fly or lure used (if desired) surrounding a dazzling silk-screened BASS or TROUT tailing on a splash of water.

Special Holiday Pricing!

This is *the* perfect gift to commemorate your angler's "FIRST" or "TROPHY" catch for only **$34.95** (**$44.95** for International Orders), shipping and handling included!

http://www.fishing.com/thank-u/
The world is your oyster, or even your bass or trout, when it comes to business on the Web. If you've got a product, the Net's got a buyer, somewhere.

not a bad deal for a device that could respond to perhaps 10,000 calls like yours in the course of that time.

Orion, of course, is not charging for this service and a paid-for magazine probably couldn't use the autoresponder approach, as the system would cheerfully dish out copies to anyone who asked for them. But charging a subscription or cover price is not the only way to derive income from a newsletter. On the Net, there is usually more than one way to skin a cat.

➡ TRUSTING THE TRIPOD

The Internet is going to demolish many well-established industry conventions and rules of thumb about what resources certain types of project require and how long they will take. It is going to make it possible for a truly global car firm, for example, or a pharmaceuticals or consumer electronics company that sets itself up with three R&D units in the right places, to cut development times on important projects by two-thirds.

Many organisations talk about the crucial importance of the 'time-to-market' factor. Now we'll see who's really serious. A company in London will simply hand the work-in-progress back a few time zones at 6 p.m. to a team of bright-eyed developers in California, who have just come in after a run on the beach and a leisurely breakfast. They will beaver away for eight hours or so and then hand on again to another team in Tokyo, Calcutta or Perth, who will work flat out on the project until it is time to pass it back again to London. The London squad will come in to work to find the development of their design or their software has come on in leaps and bounds, advancing effectively two whole days while they relaxed, recharged the batteries and slept a single night. This will be made possible by the use of Net-based videoconferencing, e-mail and huge, shared Web-style intranet sites, which are like private, in-house Internets. Crucially, with one intranet instantly accessible to all the offices, people can be sure a single update is enough to alert all three teams to any changes, making it feasible to work like this without the risk of the project collapsing into chaos.

It is obvious that this implementation approach would be a possibility for a multinational corporation such as Honda, Ford, Volkswagen or IBM. Is it so obvious, yet, that a small English software company with modest offices in Britain and America, for example, could gain a massive competitive advantage by setting up the third leg of the tripod in Australia or the Far East and making this way of working an almost unbeatable selling point in bidding for high-priority, high-value projects?

➡ CHANGING THE WAY WE WORK

Here, as a quick *hors d'oeuvre*, are six examples of how the Internet will change the way we work, at an accelerating pace, over the next few years. There will be many more.

1. We'll be instantly and intimately connected to our suppliers and customers. They will want our attention here and now or they'll go somewhere else.
2. Anyone will be able to invade our territory. Traditional strength in a market will count for little, as newcomers find barriers to entry are fewer and lower.
3. It will become impossible to push up margins, when everyone's price is so visible.
4. New laws and bodies, organised at an international level, will be needed to prevent fraud, copyright theft and serious invasions of people's privacy.
5. We will all commute less and travel to fewer meetings, as online videoconferencing finally becomes an affordable option.
6. Trade barriers, customs duties and sales taxes will come under severe pressure, as companies and consumers search for bargains around the world.

The consequences of this kind of radical change will be huge. Just how big, no-one can say. But anyone who has read this book will certainly be ahead of the game in recognising what's going on and how its ramifications are likely to develop.

➡ CHANGING THE WAY WE LIVE

People in Britain are so used to paying through the nose for everything that it hardly hurts any more. Compared with the best prices obtainable in the USA, Europe or even Japan for various goods and services, day-to-day shop prices in the UK are just too high. This is another area in which the arrival of the Internet and the World Wide Web may, with luck, have substantial knock-on effects.

British consumers pay too much for almost everything – for their cars and CDs, their electrical and electronic goods, supermarket food, pensions, insurance policies, computers, software, perfume, air tickets, shoes, jeans, beer, mobile phone calls and imported branded goods – while hardly noticing the cartels and price-fixing deals that make a mockery of the abolition of resale price maintenance more than twenty years ago.

The Office of Fair Trading and the Monopolies and Mergers Commission seem to need to catch the culprits in a price-rigging deal red-handed, clutching smoking pistols and surrounded by a mass of incriminating documentation, before any action can be taken. Press campaigns, notably some brilliant undercover work by *Sunday Times* reporters, have exposed the illegal practices of manufacturers who refuse to supply goods to outlets that will not promise to sell at the inflated prices the makers dictate. But nothing changes. It seems as if only a mass movement of shoppers voting with their feet – perhaps led by a trusted non-governmental body such as the Consumers' Association – is ever likely to bring about a radical revision of price levels.

What the Internet offers is a way to break the power of local monopolists and price-fixers by letting consumers know what people in other countries are paying and, in many cases, letting them choose to buy from suppliers overseas. Anything that can be digitised – software programs and photo library images now, but increasingly music and soon whole feature films – will be turned into a stream of bytes and downloaded over the Net from, presumably, the cheapest supplier anywhere in the world. And it's interesting to consider whose sales tax and customs regime a transaction might fall under, if it involved a consumer in Britain buying a piece of American software that was downloaded from a server in Chile or Taiwan, especially when you take into account that there need be no physical manifestation at all of either its arrival or its departure. The White House has been saying for some time that the Internet should be a tax-free zone, though what the politicians think they mean by that is anyone's guess. What may well happen is that it becomes a tax-free trading zone for disembodied objects, simply because there is no possible way of keeping tabs on what on earth's going on.

➡ A LOCAL CALL TO THE WORLD

With cars, beer, jeans and computers, where we need to receive atoms, rather than bytes, the delivery mechanisms won't be so slick. But knowing what price deals are on offer elsewhere will give us choices about whether we pay what we are asked at home or start checking taxes and shipping costs with a view to bringing the goods in from abroad.

Near-perfect knowledge of world prices will steer us towards something much closer to a perfect market, based on perfect information. This will quickly have the effect of bringing air fares in Europe down to earth, as it is already doing in the USA, and it will certainly help to put pressure on the telecommunications companies to lower their rates for mobile, national and international calls. In fact, though, the Internet is going to deal the international phone call cartels – with their artificial 'accounting rates' and 'correspondent relationships' – an even more savage and direct blow, by knocking the bottom out of overseas call prices.

Because Internet links are independent of distance, it costs us no more to visit a Website in Hawaii than one in Jerez or Hamburg or Hull. In the same way, telephony over the Internet, which is just beginning to become widely available, means you can talk to someone on the other side of the world for as long as you like, for the cost of a local call. At first, the telecoms giants reacted predictably, muttering that voice-over-IP (phoning on the Internet) meant very low quality, suitable only for impoverished students and, as one senior manager put it, 'No better than a mobile phone'. But nine million people in Britain choose to use mobile phones and an awful lot of families with Internet access have friends and relations in Australia, New Zealand, Canada or the States. So the other reaction from the telcos was just as unsurprising: they were falling over themselves to test and pilot their own voice-over-IP systems, just to be on the safe side.

Deutsche Telekom, already the largest telephone company and the largest Internet provider in Europe, broke ranks early by saying it would provide Internet phone services as part of its portfolio. It was followed in July 1998 by the surprise announcement from AT&T and BT that they were merging their international operations in a $10 billion venture to create a new global network with huge, 200 gigabits per second backbone links connecting the 100 cities that generate 90 per cent of the world's business telecommunications revenue – all based on software-driven Internet technology. This is a far cry from cheap, blurry calls for students. And now the genie is out of the bottle, it is certainly unlikely that anyone will succeed in corking it up again. It may take a while, but international call charges are about to come down and stay down for ever, thanks to the Internet.

➡ ROBOTS HELP REWRITE THE RULES

In every area, greater consumer knowledge of the relevant facts, starting with prices, will mean greater consumer power. Even the job of finding the best deals on the Web is now in the process of being automated, with the arrival of software robots, known as 'intelligent agents'. These little agents have names like WebFerret, NetAttache and Bargain Finder Agent, and clamber tirelessly around the Web on your behalf, scouring sites, directories and databases to find the cheapest items that meet the detailed specifications you have entered into their interrogation forms (including credit terms, guarantees and all the other elements you decide to rate as important). The first agents were clumsy, but they are becoming more sophisticated and useful all the time, and technical developments such as the introduction of XML, the new Extended Mark-up Language for Web text, are accelerating this process. XML automatically indicates if a certain set of numbers in a table or a piece of running text is a price (for example, recognising whether 12.30 means £12.30 or nearly lunchtime), making it easier for an intelligent agent to compare this with other prices it has found and return to base with usable information.

It is almost impossible to imagine how different life could be in a situation where all prices were transparent, based on near-perfect information and, in many cases, lower. For consumers, it is hard to see a downside. For many companies, however, it will mean that finding new ways to add real value becomes a key priority. Customers will insist on straight trade-offs between price and the extras and intangibles bundled into a deal. Retailing will undergo the biggest shake-up it has seen for several decades and many intermediaries – wholesalers, agents, brokers, distributors and dealers – will have to do some radical rethinking or be left high and dry.

It seems strange that all this is starting to come about because a few students and particle physicists bumbled their way towards inventing some new bits and pieces to hang on the ends of a creaking international telephone system. It is strange, too, that the sudden acceleration in the pace of this revolution has been fired by the World Wide Web, which is scarcely more worldwide than baseball's World Series (did you know, for example, that little Estonia has more Web servers than the whole of sub-Saharan Africa, apart from South Africa?) and is strongly biased towards the English-speaking nations. But there is a revolution and it is throwing into question many of the rules and relationships that have shaped our lives and the way we do business. The result is a wealth of new openings and opportunities, for both new and established firms and for the people who can imagine new products and services.

Exactly 100 years ago, in 1899, Charles H. Duell, the US Commissioner of Patents, announced 'Everything that can be invented has been invented.' In the light of the technological power and the seething richness of resource, ingenuity and diversity the Internet has given us to draw on, we have every chance of proving him wrong, yet again.

Chapter 2
Living in another world

'You can't discover new lands without consenting to lose sight of the shore.'

(Andre Gide, 1925)

➡ WELCOME TO VIRTUAL CANADA

There is always room for argument about how many people are connected to the Internet and how many are actively logging on and using it on a regular basis. Despite all the loose talk, the Internet population is not a separate cyber-nation of thirty, forty or eighty million people, but a widely dispersed and highly selective subset of the real population that business deals with in the physical world. That is what makes the commercial opportunities seriously interesting. For all practical purposes, it doesn't matter, yet, whether the virtual country you are addressing is the size of Canada or Spain or Germany. Plenty of businesses and plenty of personal fortunes have been built on success in national markets a good deal smaller than this. A Virtual Canada is a proposition that's worthy of anybody's attention.

The demographics of this newborn country are interesting, too. The population, at present, is affluent, predominantly middle class and English-speaking and strongly weighted towards educated young adults, with a large rising generation of Web-conscious teenagers. While one person in two of the six billion men and women on the world's surface has yet to enjoy the experience of his or her first telephone call, access to the Internet automatically means that you have passed the kind of wealth test that puts you among the richest 2 per cent or so of the human race. In terms of freedom from the threat of famine and dysentery and availability of high disposable income to spend on posh frocks, swanky cars, double CDs and interactive games, this is the marketing department's dream population.

There is a slightly lopsided look to it, as yet, which would be more worrying in a real country's population profile, because of the way Virtual Canada's gender balance is skewed towards males. This is likely to shift as access to the Web becomes more routine, ubiquitous and straightforward. There are precedents. In the early 1980s, almost all modem users were men. When fax machines came along, each with its 9600 bps modem tucked away inside and operated by pressing buttons marked '*START*' and '*STOP*', rather than typing in Hayes command codes, the number of women using modems rapidly overtook men, though the number who wanted or needed to know about the workings of the modem inside the fax was rightly tiny. Once the technology is tamed so that it helps, rather than getting in the way, there is no reason to believe the gender balance on the Internet will be anything far off 50/50.

➡ HOW BIG COULD THIS GET?

It was only in 1991 that the rules about using the Internet were altered to allow business to tiptoe onto the Net for the first time. Until then a stern 'Acceptable Use Policy' ruled out any attempt to exploit the network for profit. Indeed, it was not until 1994 that the number of businesses on the Web finally outstripped the number of educational establishments (recognisable by the .edu and .ac.uk tags). As the number of people and companies connected to the Internet spiralled into the realms of the unknowable, so did the enthusiasts' estimates of how much business on the Web could be worth.

The truth is, nobody knows – and few people have any very informed basis on which to make a guess. The US Commerce Department stuck its neck out in April 1998 with a 300-page report, entitled *The Emerging Digital Economy*, that endorsed a prediction by the Boston-based Forrester Research (*http://www.forrester.com*) that business-to-business transactions on the Net would be worth $327 billion by 2002. Like all such spuriously precise estimates, that one needs to be taken with a massive pinch of salt. Set it against the forecast of $750 billion by the year 2000 from Nicholas Negroponte, the eminent head of MIT's Media Lab, and it is clear that everyone is guessing wildly. You can join in and think of a figure, if you like. Your guess is about as likely to be right as anyone else's.

There are a few verifiable figures that are generally accepted as giving some pointers about the scale of things to come. Cisco, for example, one of the leaders in electronic commerce, is quoted by Negroponte as selling £3.5 billion-worth of big-ticket IT, networking and communications equipment a year online. Dell's direct sales of its computers across the Internet are now worth around $5 million a day, and accelerating fast. So the potential is there for big businesses to grow bigger, for IT companies to sell IT kit and for those who live and work with the Net to buy and sell things on it. That hardly counts as a surprise. But these are not the big issues. We are stumbling around in the Gutenberg and Caxton era of this technology. All our best guesstimates are likely to be as accurate and useful as the figures you'd get if you asked Caxton to predict sales figures for Dickens' novels and the *International Herald Tribune*. Until we have some idea how firmly the Internet is going to implant itself in the mainstream of our daily lives, no-one can come up with numbers that mean anything much.

Will online ordering be part of our weekly food shopping pattern? Is your refrigerator going to be wired to the Web? Will Internet videoconferencing become the usual way for grandparents to keep in touch with the children? Will the High Street be full of charity shops where the travel agents, estate agents, record shops and insurance brokers used to be? This is the sort of question that will determine whether the Web is a useful, but marginal, technology or a revolutionary factor that will reshape our days. William Gibson, the author who coined the term 'cyberspace', calls it 'a new kind of civilisation'. If he's right, guessing in the dark about just how many billion dollars Internet business may be worth in three or four years' time is probably not the most productive way for us to use our energy now.

➡ DID SOMEONE SAY 'JUST DO IT'?

All the best learning comes from doing. The way to get a feel for what the Internet and the World Wide Web can do is to plug in, turn on and explore for yourself – either randomly or following up some of the suggestions offered in this book. By far the best and cheapest way to go about this is to use someone else's computer and connection time and pick someone else's brain, either at work or away from it. It takes so little time and effort to learn the basics that this needn't be much of an imposition, and most experienced Internet users are quite happy to share their knowledge with newcomers. After visiting a few Websites and tracking down a few nuggets of information or searching for people's e-mail addresses, you will already be feeling quite at home with this easy, unintimidating technology. You will be getting occasional glimpses of how resources such as e-mail and the Web could be useful in a business context and possibly for home use, too. It is sometimes hard for the experienced user to remember the sense of excitement and dawning potential that is an almost universal reaction to that first contact with the distance-shrinking, clue-chasing, intoxicating and effortless power at your fingertips.

Assuming you already have access to a PC running Windows 95, 98 or, less ideally, 3.1, your initial encounters with the Web are almost certain to lead you on to think about the relatively small step of getting onto the Net in your own right. At this point, Mac owners may already be reaching for their pens to write complaining letters to our publishers, but we are honestly not being Mac-ist here or elsewhere in this book. Macintoshes are smashing machines, and you can connect to the Net with an Apple in exactly the same way any Windows PC user would. Indeed one of the great virtues of the browser concept is that it is platform-independent – you can use a browser to get onto the Web from a PC, an Apple, a Unix machine or almost anything. But the truth is that well over 90 per cent of all business and home Internet users are on PCs and our readers will reflect that overwhelming dominance. Simply for brevity, therefore, we will just refer to PCs, though almost everything in the book applies just as much to Mac users. It is one of our aims to minimise the importance of the hardware and emphasise that it's the ideas that count. What you and your company get out of the Internet will depend on what you choose to do with it.

If your machine does not have an internal modem, you would have to pay out about £90 for a good external unit, but there would not necessarily be any other expenses involved. Many of the biggest and most popular companies offering connection to the Internet (AOL, CompuServe, Virgin Net, BT Internet, Demon, Easynet and others) offer free introductory trials, usually for 30 days (though Which? Online, run by the Consumers' Association, currently gives you up to 59 days free), and these are so much a part of the industry's marketing stance that you need feel no compunction about trying several before you make your choice. The only minor snag is the fact that your e-mail address will be different with each provider, which may lead to some confusion among your contacts, if you skip round a number of companies.

➡ HOOKING UP TO THE WORLD

The simplest form of connection to the Internet is a dial-up link, through a modem, to an Internet service provider, or ISP. For millions of individuals and home-based businesses, the subscription of £10 to £15 a month to the service provider ($20 in the USA), in return for unlimited access to the Net is one of the bargains of the age. In America, where local calls are free, there is nothing more to pay. In the UK, the only extra expense is likely to be the cost of local-rate phone calls to the ISP's contact number. And it's getting cheaper all the time. BT now offers BT Click+ (*http://www.btclickplus.com*), a pay-as-you-go service with no fees apart from an extra 1 pence per minute on top of your local call charges, while the Dixons group's Freeserve (*http://freeserve.net*) costs nothing at all – though technical support is £1 per minute.

There are two ways of choosing a service provider. One is to pore over the detailed rankings given in the Internet magazines, comparing reliability records, data transfer speeds, ease of use ratings, uptime percentages and ratios of numbers of modems available to numbers of subscribers using them. The other is to talk to a few friends and colleagues who are using different ISPs and see if they are happy with the service they are getting. You do not need to commit yourself to an ISP for life. Nor do you need to relate on a particularly intimate level. If you don't really notice your service provider is there, between you and the Web, then the service is almost certainly good. It is worth remembering that the approach to choosing that involves examining the technical evidence is not really any more scientific than asking your friends. The scores quoted in the magazines are likely to be derived from nationally sampled data, or sometimes from research that is limited to one or two large metropolitan areas. Subjective reactions from people living near you may be difficult to calibrate, but they do represent the actual conditions prevailing in your area.

The number of service providers you have to choose from is going down all the time, as the back-bedroom enthusiasts with their home-brew ISPs find they simply can't compete with big players such as BT Internet, Global Internet, UUNet, Demon Internet and Netcom. These companies can offer faster and more direct connections to the global Internet backbone, easy-to-use software to get you connected and extensive technical support. Subscriptions to the big ISPs come with CD-ROMs containing Web browsers and an assortment of useful Internet software programs. They usually offer multiple e-mail addresses, too, allowing incoming e-mail to be streamed easily to different departments or offices.

➡ LOOKING FOR ADDED VALUE

The alternative approach to dial-up access is via the value-added services, often referred to as online services. These include providers such as AOL, CompuServe, Microsoft Network, LineOne and Which? Online. These may be slightly more expensive than straight ISPs, though several offer economical unlimited access deals: AOL's one-year unlimited package, for example, works out at less than £15 a month. As well as a link to the Internet, e-mail addresses and Web space, these companies offer their subscribers exclusive material that ordinary Internet subscribers can't reach, including news, finance and sport channels, business and travel databases, discussion forums, classified advertisements and various reference sources, on their own networks, separate from the Internet, or on special Websites that can only be accessed with a password. The advantage of this route is that you enter cyberspace in a simple, structured way, with a certain amount of useful handholding that shields you from the anarchic nature of the big, wide Internet itself. The disadvantages tend to stem from the fact that all the extra material you are offered is in a private space of its own, separate from the Internet, and that connecting through to the Web can sometimes be awkward or long-winded.

http://www.aol.com
Formerly America Online, but now with the world in its sights, AOL is the mother of all Internet gateways, with more than 13 million subscribers

All the online services have their own peculiarities. Until recently, CompuServe's two million or so members around the world had to put up with an appalling system of e-mail addresses, under which numbers were used, instead of names. So the equivalent of *fbloggs@aol.com* or *john.doe@virgin.net* would have been something like *98765.432@compuserve.com*. In 1997, Compu-Serve suddenly realised this system produced deeply unmemorable and impersonal addresses and introduced a more conventional addressing scheme, alongside its beloved numerals, which allowed members to choose names. Overnight, *98765.432@compuserve.com* could reinvent himself as *lancelot@compuserve.com* and transform his public e-image.

AOL, the biggest of the lot, with about 13 million members, has been the slowest to come round to the idea of moving its material off its private network and out onto a Website. It has also clung on to its own idiosyncratic e-mail program, which is friendly enough and easy to use, but leaves it out of step with most of the rest of the world, which has gone over to the POP3 e-mail standard. POP3 allows you to collect and send e-mail easily from almost anywhere on the planet where you can get full Internet access. Other ISPs and online services are almost unanimous in their enthusiasm for POP3 and even CompuServe, which has stuck with its own proprietary e-mail program, has now conceded that building in POP3 compatibility is a must for its members and especially important for those who are far from home and trying to retrieve mail under less than ideal circumstances.

LineOne is backed by BT, United News & Media and the Murdoch media empire, is wholly Web-based and offers full Internet access, POP3 e-mail and a fair spread of news, sport and financial information. Unlike the other major online services, it is a purely UK-centred operation, though people outside Britain can subscribe to a content-only package. The full LineOne service offers two or three pricing options, including a £15-a-month unlimited access package.

➡ **A WIDER PIPE?**

The problem with ordinary dial-up access to the Internet, for all but the smallest businesses, is that it is simply too slow and too limiting to allow anything other than the occasional peep into the potential of the world outside. One-man-band microbusinesses may find dial-up adequate. But anyone who is going to be at all serious about tracking down information, exploring market opportunities or establishing a presence on the Web is going to need a better connection.

Even at a data transfer rate of 56 Kbps (kilobits per second), the current practical maximum (and faster than many service providers can match), you will be spending too much time waiting for things to happen. A single letter or digit takes up to ten bits to transfer, so a totally glitch-free 56 Kbps should theoretically translate into roughly 5600 characters, or, say, 1100 words, or, perhaps, three A4 pages per second. That sounds quite impressive, but real-world speeds are always lower and the complex graphics, photographs, video inserts, animations and sound effects that add punch to today's Websites all soak up bits by the fistful.

More bandwidth – the ability to push more bits per second down a wider telecommunications pipe – is necessary to minimise unproductive waiting and to take account of the fact that more than one person at a time may need to be using the Internet link.

The first place to turn for advice on improving your connection to the Web is your service provider, who will be able to make an informed guess at how much capacity you need, based on information from you about your activities and practical experience of what works in actual business situations. Your ISP will question you about the number of users and how often they are likely to connect to the Net and will point out the need to network your Internet connection to make it available at the desk to different people in your team.

After scribbling sums on the back of an envelope, the expert will probably suggest either putting in a digital telephone connection (known as an ISDN line, which actually stands for Integrated Services Digital Network, but until recently was widely translated as Interesting Solution Desired by No-one) or creating a permanent, 24-hour-a-day link to the Net by installing a leased line. An ISDN line can give you increased capacity (up to 128 Kbps) and almost instant connections – two or three seconds, compared with up to 30 for ordinary dial-up service. Rental costs may be considerably higher than you are used to for an ordinary phone line (at the time of writing, BT had just introduced a Low Start Business Highway package, with a start-up fee of £149 and a rental of £88 per quarter) and you will need a more expensive gadget called a terminal adapter, instead of a modem.

Leased lines, also known as private circuits, involve paying a fixed fee for exclusive use of your own circuit, after which all your calls are free. The connection is instantaneous and the circuit capacity can be whatever your business is likely to need and is prepared to pay for. In the end, of course, there is no practical limit to the capacity that's available, at a price, even with today's technology. And with some of the new options that will become available very soon, the cost of high-speed, super-quality access is destined to fall to levels almost every business can afford. The bigger question is likely to be whether you can afford to wait for prices to come down, if there are opportunities now, in your industry, that others will be equally keen to grasp.

Chapter 3
Something for nothing

'Communication is civilisation itself. The word, even the most contradictory word, preserves contact. It is silence that isolates.'

(Thomas Mann, 1924)

➡ THE CINDERELLA SYSTEM

E-mail is fantastic. It's not glamorous, compared with the all-singing, all-dancing, dazzling, colourful, animated, hyperlinked magic of the Web. But it is, to all intents and purposes, something for nothing – or as near as you'll ever get in a business context.

E-mail is usually delivered more or less instantaneously, to anyone with an e-mail address, anywhere on earth. It costs pennies to use and demands no skill or technical knowledge. It allows you to send a message to ten people, or a hundred, or a thousand, in a matter of seconds, for a cost per head that's infinitesimal. You could e-mail every branch of a worldwide organisation, or an army of customers on five continents, for less than the cost of one postage stamp.

Stepping up a gear, you could invest a couple more minutes in the process and send a spreadsheet, a computer program, a scanned photograph or an advertising layout to each of these people, attached to your e-mail. Your attachment can be any kind of computer file, though e-mail is not always the best way to handle big, fat files of more than about 100 Kb and some company systems are set to reject large attachments, for fear of clogging up. That still gives you plenty of scope, though – in terms of word processed documents, 100 Kb would be at least two whole chapters of this book. And all you need to do to hook an attachment like this on to your e-mail is locate the file you want to send and press a single button.

The medium of e-mail is so cheap and so simple, with such amazing firepower and such low barriers to entry, that it was bound to be misused. It has been, too. 'Spamming', the sending out of thousands of items of unwanted junk e-mail to unsuspecting people whose addresses have appeared on a mailing list somewhere, was a trick many unscrupulous or overenthusiastic people tried, as a way of promoting their businesses, in the early days of the Internet.

At first, there seemed to be no way of stopping this practice – after all, the Internet is a great big, amorphous, unpoliced and unpoliceable tangle and it seemed as if there was nothing a few angry netizens could do. Then someone came up with the idea of 'mail-bombing' the culprits. This involved tracking down the e-mail address of the spam factory, the source of the junk e-mail, and sending it thousands upon thousands of meaningless or vindictively phrased e-mails – such a huge volume that it was calculated to crash the sinner's Internet server or, at the very least, choke his or her electronic mailbox. The beauty of it was that someone with 4000 angry e-mails and one reply from a client sitting in the mailbox would have to weed carefully through 4001 messages, checking before deleting each one, in order to be sure that the business baby was not being thrown out with the backlash bathwater. Spamming still happens. It is like a virus that won't entirely go away, whatever the drug companies invent, and it will be a matter of concern to governments, ISPs and businesses for years to come. But there are various partial answers to the problem, like anti-spam filter software (get it free via *http://www.pureamiga.co.uk/spam/*), and at least it doesn't occur on a scale that threatens to make the whole Internet grind to a halt, as some people feared it would.

You, of course, would only ever think of using the power of e-mail responsibly, to send relevant information to people who had demonstrated a desire to receive it. You might want to use it to cut across time-zones and leave a message for your office in New Zealand that your people could act on immediately, so that there was a positive reply waiting for you when you came into the office the next day. You might use it to react quickly to a supply shortfall and invite a dozen companies to send in instant tenders for the materials needed to plug the gap. It is certainly playing a major part in many companies' moves towards just-in-time stocking and manufacturing. You might want to join a specialist mailing list discussion group about your industry or discipline, exchanging information with others via e-mail to help you keep abreast of technology and other developments. Or you might simply want to use e-mail as a cheap, robust and practical tool for all kinds of general business communications, within your company and outside.

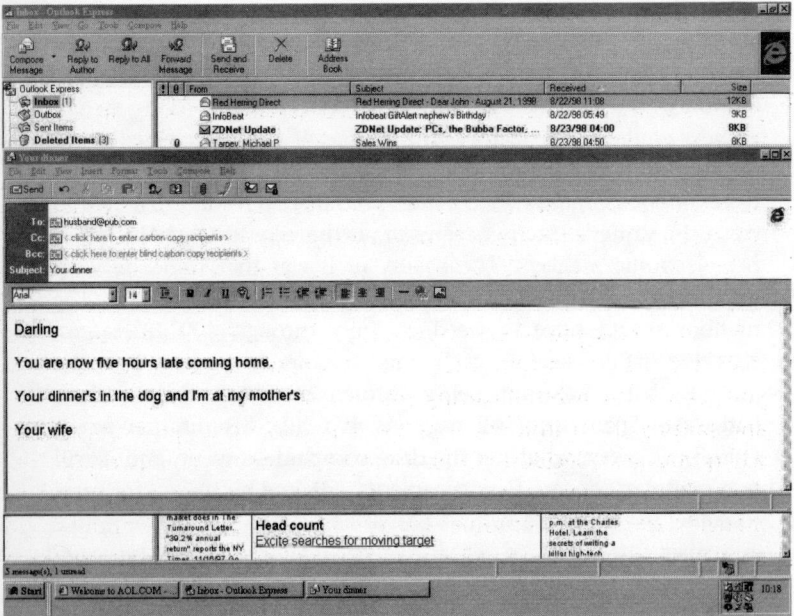

Free for all: the wonders of e-mail allow you to get the message across in an instant, at minimal cost and to any number of people

➡ **LEARNING THE BASICS IS A 10-MINUTE JOB**

You may have noticed that we have not yet started to tell you anything at all about how to connect up and make e-mail work for you. There is a reason for this. While there are many things in life – like your tax form, replacement remote controller instructions for your television, the more arcane laws of cricket and the etiquette for addressing the great and the good – which seem to be designed to cause bafflement, e-mail is generally very straightforward.

Whatever Internet service provider or online service you have subscribed to and whatever browser you are using, it's all fairly simple. You click on a button marked 'e-mail' or an envelope icon and something happens. A form, of one sort or another, opens up on your screen. At the top, there'll be a slot marked 'To:', which will give you a strong hint that that's where the e-mail address you're sending to goes. Then there will be a panel, which will fill itself in automatically, labelled 'From:'. Your e-mail address will pop up there. Ignore the CC, BCC and 'attachments' slots for the moment, put a couple of words in the 'Subject:' space, labelling the message in a way that might be useful when it comes to identifying it later, and then start writing your message in the big box underneath.

When you have finished, you will naturally want to send your e-mail winging on its way. We would recommend, however, that you get into the habit of writing your e-mails before you go online and putting them in a queue to be sent, all in one quick burst, when you next decide to connect to the Internet. This is easily done. Browsers and e-mail programs often offer you a button marked 'Send later'. On some, you will have to click on 'Options' and check a box marked 'Deferred transmission' or something similar, while others (including the popular Eudora program) just apply a bit of electronic common sense and automatically queue any e-mails you try to send while you are not connected. When you go online, you open up Eudora's 'File' menu and click on 'Send queued messages' and your volley of e-mails is unleashed on the world in a matter of seconds.

Handling outgoing e-mails this way means that your online time is kept to the very minimum. And since there is never any charge at all for actually using e-mail, the only costs involved are for the telephone connection and any online time charges levied by your service provider. Even online services like AOL, on their least economical low-user tariffs, only charge around £2.35 per hour, so the cost of sending your batches of e-mail is always going to be negligible.

➡ HANDLING INCOMING E-MAIL

Like other data on the Internet, every e-mail message that's sent to you travels across the network of networks as a series of tiny information packets, each parcelled up and addressed separately.

It makes no difference at all whether they all take the same path from A to B or whether some of them travel along a completely different route and arrive there in the wrong order. When the packets land in your mailbox, your own electronic pigeonhole on one of the computers belonging to your Internet provider, the message is reassembled and stored there until you log on and click on 'Get mail', 'Read mail', 'Mailbox: in' or something like that. You will then see a list of new messages, each with the sender's name and the subject of the message, and you can choose to click on an item to read it there and then or wait and come back to it later.

If your e-mail has been sent to you with an attachment – a scanned-in picture, a spreadsheet or a word processed document, perhaps – you will usually be offered the choice of downloading it now or later. Bear in mind that it might take several minutes to download a photograph or a substantial report. It may be better, once you have read through the covering letter, to leave the attachment in the mailbox for a while and deal with it when you are less busy. Messages and attachments can safely be left in your mailbox on the server for weeks, rather than days, as long as it doesn't get too full. To avoid this problem, you should delete mail from the mail server after you have collected it. If your mailbox does become clogged with too much old mail, all your new incoming e-mail messages will simply be bounced back to the people who have sent them.

➡ GILDING THE LILY

There are all sorts of refinements and complications available to you, once you begin to use e-mail regularly. Most of them are obviously sensible ideas, like the facility to compile an address book, so that you do not have to look up the e-mail address and type it in again every time you write an e-mail to one of your regular contacts. You have the useful ability to send multiple copies of your e-mail to other people, with or without letting people see who else is receiving it. And you can respond decisively and almost instantly to an e-mail you have just received and read, just by clicking on the 'Reply' command. This automatically sets up a new message with your correspondent's address in the 'To:' slot and the original message's title in the 'Subject' space, preceded by 'Re:'. The text of the message you are replying to is quoted in full, in brackets, and all you have to do is add your comments and send it back.

It's very quick and easy, even if, in the wrong hands, it can sometimes result in great long and winding e-mails that contain the fossilised history of an eight or nine-part rally, as people debate the pros and cons of a project. This is not inevitable, though. The quoted sections can be edited at any time and pruned back to cover just what is useful, and the quoting mechanism itself can be turned on and off at will.

All these extras are helpful, rather than essential, and are the sort of things that people learn most readily by discovering them for themselves or by talking to friends and colleagues who have had more e-mailing experience. There are plenty of books around now with laboured, step-by-step instructions on how to perform these operations, but every one of these programs offers a comprehensive on-screen 'Help' facility – and at least the help you get from this source is guaranteed to relate to the particular software and version number you are using.

➡ JUST A COUPLE OF DRAWBACKS

Whatever people think they are going to get from the Internet, e-mail is the one facility that always seems to exceed their expectations. When consumer groups run user test panels for Internet beginners, before-and-after surveys invariably show that e-mail has won over many of the doubters and technophobes with its speed, simplicity and convenience. People who haven't had access to it before soon wonder how they ever managed without it.

But there are still gaps to be plugged and you have to be realistic about them. E-mail is one of the oldest methods of communication on the Internet and there are some aspects of it that have not been brought entirely up to date. More than two decades since the first computer networks that eventually evolved into the Net were built, the fundamentals of e-mail have hardly changed, though it is certainly serving millions more people and businesses now than even five years ago. Vast amounts of e-mail traffic pass across the Internet every day, yet there is still no recognised way of confirming that a particular e-mail message has reached its destination or been read. This is a major limitation in business, where the ability to piece together an audit trail or prove that an order or instruction has been received is often crucial. At the moment, no company in its right mind wants to find itself in any kind of legal action that might turn on a question of the standing of an e-mail message.

➡ HOW DO YOU FIND SOMEONE'S E-MAIL ADDRESS?

The other missing link is the fact that there is still no straightforward way of finding e-mail addresses from public sources. To start e-mailing someone, you may well have to track down a telephone number, ring him or her up and ask for the address, which is a very un-Netlike approach, but at least gives you the information you need for next time. The directories that do exist are very incomplete, tip-of-the-iceberg attempts at putting together a list, drawn from indirect sources, such as the addresses of participants in e-mail discussion groups, and from people's own submission forms. In fact, as the number of newcomers using the Internet explodes, driven by the popularity of the World Wide Web, the proportion of users who actively participate in newsgroup debates is declining. This makes newsgroups even less significant as a source of addresses. The largest databases still have only about 10 million e-mail addresses and there are several times that number of people using e-mail every week.

Your best bet for finding UK e-mail addresses is probably Bigfoot's UK directory at *http://www.bigfoot.co.uk*, the British end of one of the biggest American operations. Bigfoot claims 'the Internet's largest collection of e-mail addresses and "white pages" listings', which means, in practice, that it has compiled over 8 million e-mail addresses and 100 million phone numbers. The US e-mail champion, however, is Four11 (*http://www.four11.com*), which boasts well over 10 million e-mail addresses and offers a sensibly designed query form which immediately lets you narrow the search by giving the city, state or country of your target individual. If you are looking for John Smith, this saves you having to wait for and wade through an initial list of hundreds of

http://www.four11.com
Want to e-mail Kate Moss and ask for a date? The good news is Four 11 can help. But it's not saying which (if any) of these 22 is the real Kate

apparently suitable candidates to find the man you want. You can also enter a 'smart name' or nickname, so that if you are trying to find the right William Robinson, you can distinguish straight away between your classmate Bill Robinson and our Motown hero Smokey Robinson.

If you draw a blank with Four11 and Bigfoot, you can try WhoWhere? (*http://www.whowhere.com*), bringing together e-mail addresses, phone numbers and personal Website addresses, Info-space, which offers over 200 million telephone numbers and e-mail addresses from around the world (*http://www.infospace.com/info/people.htm*), and Internet Address Finder (IAF) (*http://www.iaf.net*), which helpfully allows the use of asterisks as wildcard characters if you are unsure about the spelling of a name. Another approach is to try 'Email Lookup' in Excite (*http://www.excite.com*) or 'People Find' in Lycos (*http://www.lycos.com*).

➡ THE WORLD'S LARGEST E-MAIL ADDRESS BOOK

The best tactic of the lot, however, may be to go German. MESA, the Meta Email Search Agent (*http://mesa.rrzn.uni-hannover.de/*), is run by the Computer Center of Lower Saxony at the University of Hanover (or 'Hannover', as the Germans will insist on calling it) and claims to be the world's largest e-mail address book. It allows a single entry (mandatory last name, optional first name and specified maximum searching time, in seconds) to start a parallel search of Four11, Bigfoot, IAF and Infospace, plus Swissinfo, Populus and suchen.de, the main e-mail search engine for Germany. This is an impressive service – quick to load, functional and covering a lot of ground. No-one else hooks you up to so much search engine power in one go, though 555–1212.com (*http://www.555-1212.com/email.htm*), which is primarily a telephone directory, offers you the convenience of three useful query forms at once, for Four11, WhoWhere? and IAF.

For the full FAQ (frequently asked questions) run-down on the art of e-mail address hunting, go to *http://www.qucis.queensu.ca/FAQs/email/finding.html* at Queen's University, Kingston, Ontario. This even includes advice on searching some of the neglected and near-obsolete pre-Web backwaters of the Internet, where you may find dusty e-mail addresses that have lain undisturbed for years.

If you get an e-mail address wrong, incidentally, you will receive a warning message in your mailbox saying that your e-mail cannot be delivered. The first thing to do is check that you have entered the address correctly, with no spaces between characters, with no accidental comma where the dot should have been and with any capital letters in the right places. E-mail addresses are almost always lower case, but some mail systems are case-sensitive, just to make life interesting. If you have simply made a typing error or the address no longer exists, the system will let you know very promptly, within a few minutes. Occasionally, though, a message may be returned to you after two or three days. This suggests that there may be problems at the other end that are making it difficult to deliver your message, such as a mail server groaning under the weight of undeleted mail. Try re-sending, and, if that doesn't work, revert to the older technologies and pick up the phone to find out what's going on.

If finding individuals' e-mail addresses is hard, life tends to be much easier with businesses. They usually want to be found and you can generally get hold of the Web and e-mail addresses you want from Yell (*http://www.yell.co.uk*), or start by finding out a company's address and phone number from Freepages (*http://www.freepages.co.uk*). Yell gives you the choice of looking for a business name in an alphabetical list or a classified category or searching for a Website through the EYP (Electronic Yellow Pages) link button, entering a location and either the company name or the type of business to begin searching. Freepages goes at it from the top down. You type in the name of a town or city, pick a business category and then wait for a listing to come back of all the firms in the area which are in that line of business.

➡ A FORUM SMALL FIRMS CAN AFFORD

E-mail also provides the platform for a great deal of discussion in which people talk about subjects close to their hearts on the Internet, through the medium of what are known as newsgroups and mailing lists. These are subtly different, but both seek to engage people with interests in an extraordinary range of topics, from archery to zoology, via left-handedness and marketing. Mailing lists have their origins in the universities, where they developed to bring academics together to discuss their esoteric specialities. You subscribe to a mailing list and receive in your mailbox every day – and in many cases, several times a day – the thoughts, opinions and prejudices of your fellow subscribers, who may number ten or 20,000. And you can usually chip in your own two-penn'orth, too, thoughtful, opinionated or prejudiced as it may be. Needless to say, the value of any information you get from a mailing list depends entirely on whether you have any reason to believe your informant is reliable, but there are certainly some highly technical and specialised lists where the standard of debate is unimpeachably high.

You can find out about lists that might interest you by contacting the biggest list of lists – amusingly named *http://www.liszt.com* – and searching by typing in an appropriate key-word. Liszt claims to be able to put you in touch with, at the time of writing, 84,792 mailing lists, yielding, for example, 71 different offerings in response to the keyword 'football', for teams ranging from the Washington Redskins (over 30 new e-mail postings a day) to Blackpool's relatively unglamorous soccer club (5 to 50 postings daily, from over 150 subscribers, 'depending on how wound-up everyone is').

Mailing lists are easy to set up for yourself, either by getting hold of the appropriate software and running the list from your own site or by renting mailing list space. Listbox (*http://www.listbox.com*) will let you set up a site for $5 to $50 (£3 to £30) a month, depending on the number of subscribers and messages involved. For the small, specialist company, owning your own mailing list on the Internet can be a useful community-building marketing tool and a valuable source of feedback – especially as it's extremely cheap and manageable. If it's your list, you can control who is accepted as a subscriber and who is allowed to post messages and you can even screen individual postings and refuse any you deem unhelpful.

Suppose, for example, that your small firm has devised a better sort of toothbrush for dogs, a revolution in canine oral hygiene, and you feel that vets and some unlucky dog owners might be particularly interested in discussing issues related to your product.

You might go to Listbox and start a mailing list called *dogbreath @listbox.com*. Anyone who wanted to subscribe would send an e-mail message addressed to *majordomo@listbox.com*, saying simply 'subscribe dogbreath myname@xxnet.com' and, unless you objected, would then start receiving all the mailing list postings. When they had had enough, or wanted to go on holiday without returning to a bulging mailbox, they would just send another message to the same address, in the form 'unsubscribe dogbreath myname@xxnet.com'.

➡ WHAT ARE YOU UP TO, MRS TIGGYWINKLE?

Though newsgroups are also a mechanism for allowing likeminded people to share their opinions, they are slightly different, in that they are maintained on your ISP's server, which gives the more prudish a chance to censor the explicitly sexual or non-politically correct newsgroups and simply not carry them. Newsgroups will probably be collected automatically in a separate part of your e-mail program, where you will find a list that can be searched in the usual way, by typing in a keyword. This is necessary, because, again, the number on offer is enormous. Global Internet, for example, has 23,000 newsgroups (79 of them, it appears, concerned with some form of fetish) from Barbie to beans and from motorbikes to Beatrix Potter.

The options for discussion and meeting likeminded people on the Net now go far beyond the e-mail-based services, extending into Web-based keyboard chat sites and bulletin boards, such as the fast-growing examples maintained by Yahoo. But in all cases, the same rules apply. A receptive scepticism is the order of the day. The information and support you can glean ranges from the amazingly useful – such as the help available for people suffering from rare diseases – to the useless and the downright dangerous.

➡ WAITING FOR THE PICTURE TO CLEAR

Mailing lists and newsgroups have been very important, over many years, in the development of the Internet as a rich, unpredictable and rewarding source of information, debate, entertainment, comfort and advice. They still are important and underpinning them is one of e-mail's major roles, alongside its bread and butter job of providing almost instant, almost costless worldwide communication.

But e-mail alone could never move the Internet as decisively towards centre stage as the Web has done in less than five years. And it is the abundant power, potential and momentum of the World Wide Web that is unleashing the real information explosion that has been so loudly heralded for two decades or more. Text alone could never do the trick. We didn't know it, but our visual, TV-bred generations were waiting for point and click, for computer communication that dealt in images, rather than words. Now it's here and the real revolution has started to roll. And we ain't seen nothing yet.

Chapter 4
The world's your library

'The searcher's eye will often find more than the searcher had in mind.'

(Gotthold Ephraim Lessing, 1779)

➡ FINDING THE DOPE

The Internet contains so much information that it's difficult to know where to start. Worse than that, it can drive you nuts. There's no handy index or telephone directory. There are no outer limits and there's no central indexer. Perhaps worst of all, there's no quality control.

The beauty is, anyone and everyone can have their tuppence worth on the Internet, whether it's really worth £2,000 or 0.2p. Take a look at the stockmarket chat boards, where investors swap stories and opinions about shares and market movements. Who's that guy trashing the stock of Amalgamated Biscuit Holdings with a rumour that they are about to recall 30 million Chocolate Twerps because of a poison scare? A whistle-blower with inside knowledge? A disgruntled ex-employee? An investor who's just sold a block of shares and wants to buy them back cheaper? All of the above? Or is he just a nutter?

The truth is, you don't know. But this man now has the platform to confuse and dismay you, the company, its shareholders, employees in eight countries and buyers of Chocolate Twerps around the world. Not bad for the price of an e-mail. For those of an anarchist disposition, the Internet is, inevitably, a happy hunting ground. In all versions of the physical world, there is some form of policing – if not by the State, then through peer group pressure. On the Net, there is no force that can prevent the madman shouting 'Fire' in a crowded theatre. The only relief is that there is no actual theatre and no-one will die in the rush for the doors. But if anyone needed proof of Francis Bacon's late 16th-century insight that 'knowledge is power', this is where to find it. The problem is not so much one of gathering information, but of knowing how to value what you have collected.

You need a hand. And there's an army of hands out there, reaching out towards you. The biggest hands come in the shape of the online services and the 'portals' – companies that are eager to meet you at the door of the Internet and show you round their different services. It's no coincidence that the best-performing Internet stocks in the boom year of 1998 included the biggest of the online services, AOL, and the best-known portal, Yahoo! (*http://www.yahoo!.com*).

➡ THE MEETERS AND GREETERS

AOL (which makes its money from subscriptions) stakes its claim via its massive non-Internet area, which provides a heavily categorised and organised route into the online universe. You do need special AOL software to see its proprietary content, but it also gives access to the full Internet world and does a reasonably effective job of bringing the two together.

Yahoo! earns its revenue from the advertisers and business partners who want to be seen by the millions of people who know and love the Yahoo! name and turn to it first when they switch on and arrive on the Net. For many, Yahoo! feels like home. You can't quite sleep in Yahoo!, but you can check your shares, send and receive e-mail, play games, find a lover and search for your friends there. Yahoo!'s roots lie in providing an easy, accessible way to locate relevant information in the vastness of the Web. But its founders were among the first to spot that providing a free guide to the World Wide Web, even for millions of users every day, wasn't the road to riches and that you needed to do a lot more in the way of building up an online community to attract advertisers and viewers.

Almost all the search engines that people turn to to help find things on the Web are now in the portal game, along with many others who see this as the best way to grab a slice of the Internet's fabled and elusive riches. Even the biggest players in town have come splashing into the same pool, led by Netscape and Microsoft. But how long this business model will continue to make sense is anyone's guess. Fashions come and go frighteningly fast in the businesses surrounding the Internet and some aspects of the next wave of technology – particularly the arrival, in numbers, of the software search robots known as intelligent agents – may make portals redundant.

➡ WHERE DOES YOUR SEARCH START?

But let's get back to the business of searching for information. The usual way to begin looking for what you want is to connect up to a search engine – a Website that's dedicated to making the link between you and the information you need. Technically, there are subtle and ever-diminishing distinctions to be drawn between search engines and directories. Search engines have software robots (also known as spiders or crawlers) that mosey around the Web, ferreting out information and reporting back to a central database, and on-screen enquiry forms that allow you to search by entering keywords relevant to your subject.

Directories do it differently, letting you progress to the area you need by working your way down a tree-diagram of branching categories and sub-categories. Their content is provided by human beings who submit details of their sites and ask for the information to be included in the directory, where it may or may not be placed in the category they would have chosen. But since the most famous directory of all, by far, is Yahoo! and that opens up with a typical search engine keyword enquiry form, as well as a list of head categories for top-down searching, you might as well forget the technicalities and think of them all as search engines. We shall certainly use the phrase quite indiscriminately throughout the rest of this book and confidently hope to survive without being struck down by a bolt of lightning.

It's hard to give generalised advice on which search engine to use without colliding head-on with people's fiercely held prejudices.

Enthusiasts have come to blows in pubs over arguments about whether Excite (*http://www.excite.com*) is more discriminating than Lycos (*http://www.lycos.com*) or whether AltaVista (*http://www. altavista.digital.com*) is likely to be a better starting point than Yahoo!. There's even a whole site (*http://www.searchenginewatch .com*) dedicated to the subject and there are certain magazines that devote pages of reviews to making fatuous comparisons between different search engines' abilities when it comes to finding sites which contain a clutch of multiple keywords like 'chicken', 'stomach', 'Wolverhampton Wanderers' and 'Zen Buddhism'.

If it's any help, when we tried this important scientific test with Lycos, HotBot and Excite, none of them could come up with a single Website that gave a 100 per cent match and contained all four of these keywords and phrases. It was Wolves that caused the problem, though. With the list narrowed down to just 'chicken', 'stomach' and 'Zen Buddhism', the search engines performed with quick and impressive agility. Both Lycos and HotBot returned details of a truly obscure personal Website in Hawaii containing the idiosyncratic diary of a youngster who appears to spend his entire time studying Japanese, playing Super Mario go-kart games on a Nintendo 64 and arguing with his friends and colleagues. Sure enough, a recent month's ramblings did include references to stomachs, chickens and Zen Buddhism, and the worldwide power and usefulness of the Web and two of its leading search engines were thus triumphantly proven. Indeed, when this book reaches the 50th State, someone is suddenly going to have his 15 minutes of fame almost literally out of the blue.

➡ A QUESTION OF TASTE

These days, our personal favourite among the major search engines is *Wired* magazine's HotBot (*http://www.hotbot.com*), though that may be largely a question of habit. For the avoidance of doubt, it should be mentioned here that the 'bot' element in many Internet-related names is merely a slightly self-conscious short form of 'robot'. HotBot gives you the ability to manipulate and narrow down your search parameters with intuitive and easy-to-use power search tools and has a particularly good reputation for homing in reliably on proper names embedded in a Website's text.

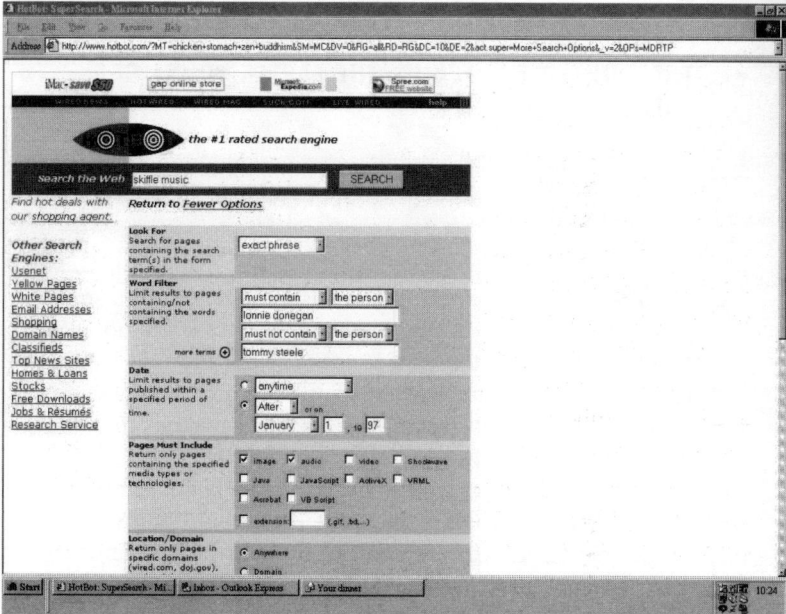

http://www.hotbot.com
It's a mighty fine line. This search on Hotbot turned up just one hit, but a good one, including an audio clip of Lonnie's own hit, Rock Island Line

On the other hand, we know people who swear by Excite – which uses a slightly different approach from its rivals, based partly on artificial intelligence techniques, and is sometimes capable of producing eerily appropriate results – and others who swear at it for coming up with what seem like bafflingly random shots.

There is also an enthusiastic faction that favours the eccentric, quick and sometimes helpful Ask Jeeves (*http://www.askjeeves.com* or even just *http://www.aj.com*). This searches several major search engines in parallel, plus its own database. It encourages questions in plain English ('Where can I find out about American dental Websites?') and has its own style of replying with more questions

('I know the answer to the following questions: Where can I get orthodontic advice online? Where can I find information about America?' and so on). Click on the nearest to your subject area and a drop-down box will offer a clutch of other potentially relevant links. It's an odd system, but it's better in practice than it sounds.

➡ THE TIGHTER THE FOCUS, THE FASTER YOU'LL GET THERE

Size isn't everything, but AltaVista (which boasts an index of over 125 million individual Web pages) and Yahoo! have the biggest, broadest general purpose databases. As anyone who uses AltaVista will know, there are few things in life more frustrating than waiting to receive your search results and then being confronted by a heading that tells you the search engine has come up with 1,128,419 results that match your keywords – oh, and here are the first 10 of them. Much of the art of using search engines and staying sane is to do with picking a bunch of keywords that will lead to the area you are interested in and nowhere else. Unusual words will obviously cut down the number of apparent hits – sites that contain your keywords – and your aim should be to group together several terms that are unlikely to occur near each other except in the context you want. Once you have thought of a few likely words, decide which of them absolutely must be included for a result to be of interest to you and enter a plus sign immediately in front of the first character of each of these essential words.

The more of your keywords you can make mandatory in this way, the less clutter and the fewer irrelevant answers will be returned by the search engine. When we were looking for reports of the Sotheby's auction of football kit and memorabilia in July 1998, timed to coincide with the World Cup finals, we hunted for information using several major search engines and submitting a group of keywords that asked for '+Sothebys +soccer July shirt'. 'Sothebys' was clearly the starting point and 'soccer' was chosen to avoid any rugby or American football connections confusing the issue, both words being labelled as 'musts' by the addition of the plus signs. 'July' and 'shirt' were words that were highly likely to appear, but not mandatory. They were included to lessen the chances of reports coming back of earlier Sothebys' sales or of auctions of football-related paintings.

http://www.elibrary.com
And the answer is the New York Yankees. Research your business plan without leaving your desk – and check your knowledge of baseball history too.

Working on the time-honoured principle of 'When all else fails, read the instructions', many people eventually get round to looking through the help and advice files provided by their favorite search engines – and often glean detailed advice that can make their searching more productive. For example, some of the search engines, including AltaVista, allow you to search for a whole phrase if you place it within double quotation marks. If the phrase is made up of several common words ('Candle in the Wind', perhaps), it is essential to steer the search away from trying to respond to the individual elements (109,717 hits for 'candle', 802,648 hits for 'wind' and 58,806 apparent matches for the two together) and to insist that it focuses on the complete phrase (just 5000 hits for "Candle in the Wind" with quotation marks).

Another crucial tip is to try using AND NOT to keep searches on target and rule out irrelevancies, especially if one of your keywords has more than one meaning. If you want to find out about a rock star's relationship with her daughter, by all means search for 'Madonna AND child', but take the trouble to add 'AND NOT Jesus AND NOT painting' to avoid being swamped with religious and artistic references. A similar result can frequently be achieved by using minus signs in front of these anti-keywords. Enter '-Jesus -painting' to ensure that you scoop up only links relating to the Material Girl and her little girl.

➡ MORE TIPS FROM THE EXPERTS

Tactics like this, that allow you to take control by narrowing the search area or anticipating unwanted responses and excluding them altogether, are becoming more and more important as the number of sites and documents on the Web doubles and redoubles.

To refine your searching techniques even further, get hold of the Web Search Cheat Sheet at *http://www.colosys.net/search* and drop in on The Spider's Apprentice, or Spidap for short, a fascinating site run by Monash Information Services in Massachusetts (*http://www.monash.com/spidap.html*). Set some time aside for your visit to Spidap, as it adds up to a quick and thorough crash course in searching, full of tips and information and written in a bright, punchy style that makes it all seem very simple. It also gives helpful advice on finding people, company information and current affairs material and on searching newsgroup discussion databases. You should also work your way through AltaVista's more formal help pages, where you will eventually come to some useful but little-known Web search techniques, such as searching for 'image:clinton' to find only pages with pictures of the man or using 'domain:uk' or 'domain:ch' to restrict a search to pages from Britain or Switzerland.

For UK-related queries, incidentally, you can often save a few seconds by jumping straight in at Yahoo!'s UK and Ireland site (*http://www.yahoo!.co.uk*), or try UKOnline (*http://www.ukonline.com*) or Yell, a surprisingly broad-ranging resource provided by BT's

Yellow Pages subsidiary (*http://www.yell.co.uk*). You can also dip into other countries' online cultures by heading off to Yahoo! France at *http://www.yahoo!.fr* or Yahoo! Deutschland, for example, at *http://www.yahoo!.de*.

Searching for answers across the largest information source in world history can be quick, stimulating and rewarding or slow, boring and frustrating. But it is worth remembering that there are usually several ways to get to the information you are seeking. Again, as with the very subjective business of choosing an Internet service provider, try a few search engines (*http://www.searchengine watch.com/facts/major.html* has a good list) and see which ones you get on best with. After all, you don't need to make any commitment or pay any money and you will undoubtedly use several of them from time to time.

➡ A SMALL INVESTMENT GOES A LONG WAY

Why would anyone want to pay for information, when there is so much of it available free on the Net? There are several answers. The first is quality. As demonstrated earlier in this chapter, some free information has negative value because you don't know who put it there or why. The second is commerce, because anyone who has information with any scarcity value is bound to want to charge for it. And the third is economy, because the Internet can make information that people are quite happy to pay for much cheaper to access than it was previously.

One of the sites that always comes as a vivid reminder of the wonders of the Web (as well as being incredibly useful in all forms of journalistic work) is Dow Jones Interactive (*http://www.djinterac tive.com*). This site gives everyone who wants it access to the huge resources of Dow Jones News Retrieval (DJNR), one of the world's great online news services, with its archived records of thousands of the world's leading newspapers and magazines.

In the bad old days, the only way you could get access to DJNR was to sign up through a local sales office. You then had to install some rather so-so software, get trained up, read a manual as thick as a bible and make yourself familiar with some pretty arcane search commands. Oh yes, and pay by the minute, story, month, year and who knows what else when the bill came thumping in.

Today, all you need to do is sign up online with a credit card for the princely sum of $30 a year (about £18, and they'll even waive that fee in year one) and then search away, clicking on all the subjects, papers and countries you want to look at. You are able to scan the headlines and the first sentence of each article free. After that, you have to pay to see the full text, though as the story fee is usually only $2.95, that is not likely to break the bank. It's anyone's guess what's happened now to the army of sales staff, support staff, software programmers and manual writers Dow Jones News Retrieval used to support … but the answer will be out there online somewhere.

Another best buy is the Electric Library (*http://www.elibrary.com*). As the e-library people themselves put it: 'With the Electric Library, any person can pose a question in plain English and launch a comprehensive, simultaneous search through more than 150 full-text newspapers, hundreds and hundreds of full-text magazines, two international newswires, two thousand classic books, hundreds of maps and thousands of photographs, as well as major works of literature and art.' All that comes to you for $10 a month or $60 (£37) a year, all-in, with no extras, service charges, VAT or sales tax. It's fantastic value. The Electric Library is slightly less business-minded and more academic and home-oriented than DJNR, but you still get a lot of bang for your bucks.

Both Dow Jones and the Electric Library offer special deals for group subscriptions and company-wide access. But if you're a young manager trying to make a name for yourself, why not take the initiative and sign up for one or both these services off your own bat? You're bound to make an impression on your bosses as you come up with the answers to obscure questions ahead of anyone else ('Who do we need to beat to break into the Latvian shoe-polish market, Jenkins?') and your annual bonus will more than cover the subscription costs.

Chapter 5
Auctions speak louder than words

'The commerce of the world is conducted by the strong, and it usually operates against the weak.'

(Henry Ward Beecher, 1887)

➡ 'WE WANT TO RETAIN SOME SEMBLANCE OF CONTROL'

If you don't believe that the Internet is going to change the rules – all the rules – look at what it can do in a market where the big players have had it all their own way for too long. Look at the business of selling air tickets.

In the past, airline ticket prices have been set by airlines. They are sophisticated businesses, with a lot of market experience, mighty reservation and information systems and effectively unlimited computing power to help them adapt and adjust their pricing models. They have become very good at selling us exactly the same product (a seat in a metal tube, flying at a set time between here and there) for whatever price we can be manoeuvred into paying.

On a scheduled transatlantic flight from London to New York, the differential between the cheapest prebooked APEX tickets and the full standard economy fare can be almost a factor of 3 – same seat, same cabin, same flight, but three times the price. It's a similar story on internal flights in America. To quote the examples used in one of the Consumer Reports newsletter's advertisements, the same trip can cost $2476, or $1733, or $900, or virtually any figure in between. It's called 'value-based pricing'. But though a policy of value-based pricing is part of every carrier's sales armoury, no-one pretends that it actually maximises the airlines' potential revenues.

There are still plenty of empty seats being flown across the continents and oceans of the world and earning nobody anything.

The Internet innovation that could knock all this nonsense sideways is a Website at *http://www.priceline.com* . On Priceline, would-be air passengers name the price they would be willing to pay for a particular journey and then sit back and wait – for a few minutes, an hour, or, for international flights, up to a day. While they wait, priceline.com burrows around and tries to match this bid with an airline that's willing to do a deal at the offer price. It works, and it has got the airlines more than a little jumpy.

Ecstatic customer feedback on priceline.com's Website tells a heartwarming tale of weddings celebrated, anniversaries enjoyed, countries visited, births unmissed, families reunited and business meetings attended. People talk of 'making reasonable offers' and 'wanting to be fair to the airlines', but report that they have been able to buy today's tickets at yesterday's prices or, in some cases, that they have acquired tickets on major carriers at not much more than half the fares they had been quoted by travel agents.

The awe at what this technology can make possible, the tone of surprise and the sense of the world having shifted slightly on its axis are unmistakable. On their own admission, many of these satisfied travellers originally responded to press coverage, or to priceline.com's radio commercials, featuring Star Trek's William Shatner, with some hesitation. After getting their tickets and completing their journeys, they are clearly enchanted with the whole philosophy of a near-perfect market, in which they effectively negotiate a win–win deal with the airline.

The airlines, however, are less enchanted. While priceline.com customers applaud the Internet for making consumer power a reality, airline executives have seen the beginning of a trend they don't like.

To hear the established carriers crying 'Foul!' is a bracing experience in itself, especially when they make specious appeals to the gods of the free market.

'It's not a traditional supply-and-demand market any more,' a senior man at Continental Airlines grumbled. 'Priceline flips the power relationship on its head, when the customer is telling you what he will pay.'

Web or no Web, no-one is forcing the airlines to make deals at below list prices. The old power relationship has not been stood on its head, since a true reversal of the previous situation would mean the customers exerting an unfair semi-monopoly power over the airlines. What the airlines find shocking is actually the introduction, for the very first time, of something approaching a supply-and-demand marketplace for their product.

The reaction of Southwest Airlines' Director of Electronic Commerce was far more candid. Quoted in *Interactive Week* in June 1998, he said: 'Priceline takes pricing and inventory control into a chaotic environment. We want to retain some semblance of control.' The potential for chaos and the challenges of dynamic inventory management are problems airlines and many other big businesses are going to have to get used to as the Internet begins to make its presence felt. But the ability to control markets – even to retain 'some semblance of control' – may be evaporating before our eyes. It's a headache for big businesses used to operating from dominating positions in highly structured markets. For consumers and small businesses, it's a revolution that can't come soon enough.

➡ PLUGGING THE GAPS IN YOUR LIFE

The strange, revolutionary beauty of the Internet is its unique ability to bring together buyers and sellers of goods and services who would never have found each other via any other route.

In theory, at least, anyone, anywhere can find out about what you have to sell. The angler in Peru can buy the hand-made Argyll socks that are normally sold over the counter in a little shop in Oban. The collector in Zimbabwe can keep an eye out for Shaker furniture passing through shops or salesrooms in Boston and Springfield. The science fiction fan in London can track down out-of-print bug-eyed monsters via the Barnes & Noble or Amazon .com sites, both covering far more titles than any physical bookshop anywhere.

All this is good business, of course, for the sellers. But it also introduces previously non-existent options and possibilities into the buyer's life. Because urban and suburban life in Western countries is so liberally supported by supermarkets, department stores and specialist shops of every kind, backed up by catalogue and mail order services, people tend to lose sight of the true joy of shopping – the satisfaction that comes from plugging some sort of gap in your life. All children know the anguish of not being able to have the toy they want or being unable to complete a collection they have set their hearts on. Blasé adults lose sight of the power of this kind of experience and come to regard shopping as a chore. Yet everyone can think of something that is no longer to hand – an old song, an obscure book with a half-remembered title, a punnet of the little, dark, strong-tasting strawberries that have been overtaken by today's plump, bland giants – that is missing, and missed, if only for nostalgic reasons. It is unlikely that any particular recording, or any book, or even any strain of strawberry, has actually vanished completely from the face of the planet. But unless you know where to begin looking for them, these experiences cannot be enjoyed again. Suddenly, with the Internet to help you, this kind of pursuit of the odd, the unfashionable, the nostalgic or the wildly idiosyncratic becomes completely feasible, and even enjoyable in its own right.

➡ THE CAR BOOT SALE GOES ONLINE

Enabling people to find the things they want that they can't get by walking into an ordinary shop is one aspect of the Internet's attraction. Enabling them to acquire goods and services they could not otherwise afford is another. It can take many forms. The ability to gather and compare instant quotes from many different sources allows consumers to shop around for bargains when they are looking for books or cars, holidays or insurance. People who need good computers but can't afford absolute leading edge technology can take advantage of manufacturers' end-of-line stock clearance sales. And though the old phrase *caveat emptor* ('buyer beware') is just as topical as ever on the Internet, there are undoubtedly millions of second-hand bargains available online. These include many items, effectively offered to a worldwide market through being advertised on the Web, that would not even justify the costs of advertising in a local newspaper.

The biggest person-to-person electronic auction site, eBay (*http://*

www.ebay.com), has become extraordinarily successful, on a scale that many people who have not sampled this online car boot sale find hard to believe. By late 1998, just three years after its launch, eBay had auctioned 25 million lots, gone public with a successful Nasdaq share offering and was claiming more than 1 million registered customers. It could boast nearly 800,000 items for sale at any one time, including antiques and collectibles, computers, books and a huge range of oddments in its 'miscellaneous' category. Auction charges for low value items have always been pitched at modest levels, so that the fees charged on something which eventually sold on a bid just below $25, for example, would be less than $1.75. At the other end of the scale, the sale of a laptop where the eventual price was $1200 would attract total charges (insertion fee plus pro rata final value fee) of $30.13, or about 2.5 per cent of the sale price.

http://www.ebay.com
If you can't find it on eBay, you're probably in a minority of one in your area of interest. This search for cushions came up with 15 plump little hits

For its fans, this is not just a new way of trading. Few people arrive, look around and leave, never to return, and the auction company's long-term intentions are clearly flagged in its tagline: 'eBay – your personal trading community'. The idea is to attract and involve people in a community that means more to them than just an opportunity to buy and sell. Both buyers and sellers are encouraged to contribute to an active feedback forum, which captures some astonishingly impassioned emotional reactions to the eBay experience. The excitement and curiosity value of involvement in an online auction are clearly attractive to many participants. But eBay also receives feedback forms that run on for page after page, with some users pouring their hearts out and declaring that the arrival of eBay has changed their lives for the better.

➡ GOING, GOING, GONE

If eBay has changed lives and started to build a new sense of community with its new approach to person-to-person, classified ads-style trading, it is not the only site that is benefiting from the Internet's unique advantages as a saleroom for electronic auctions. American sites, such as Onsale (*http://www.onsale.com*), and their British shadows, such as Quixell (*http://www.quixell.com*), have attracted a great deal of attention by auctioning PC systems, consumer electronics and other goods, often sourced directly from major brand name manufacturers. Buyers register their credit card details, view the meticulously detailed lists of goods on offer, lodge their bids and hope for the best. The bidder is tipped off by e-mail if another bid comes in at a higher level and the battle can swing back and forth, just as it would in a live auction, until the pre-arranged closing time, when the auctioneering software allocates the lot automatically to the highest bidder.

There is room for plenty of drama and excitement for the participants and the prices that are achieved clearly reflect genuine market forces at work. Onsale, in particular, has built its reputation partly on its ability to source good quality equipment, both new and refurbished, from several of the world's leading PC manufacturers. Anyone who is working on a tight budget can see the appeal of picking up, say, a one-year-old IBM Thinkpad, refurbished but backed by a newly issued 12-month IBM guarantee, at around half the original list price. It is no surprise that Jerry Kaplan, Onsale's co-founder and CEO, talks enthusiastically about the excitement and fun that seem just as important to his customers as the bargain prices. He has noticed the way people talk about their successes at auction as 'winning', as if they had hit the jackpot at Las Vegas, and he does not discount the importance of the gaming impulse in fuelling his firm's spectacular growth. Onsale claims to have registered bids from more than 600,000 bidders and is now steadily expanding its range of goods and services, from the core areas of computers, peripherals and consumer electronics into sporting goods, gourmet foods and even holidays.

➡ A CATALYST FOR CHANGE

Analysing the impact of the various Internet auction sites underlines three unique aspects of the World Wide Web:

1. It offers the chance to build a community, with shared interests and some sense of shared values, in the course of trading and doing business on the Web.

2. It poses a threat to many conventional business activities, and particularly to brokers, agents, wholesalers and other intermediaries who make their money in the space between sellers and buyers. It also implies that the traditional physical infrastructure of many businesses may no longer be necessary. (Will Christie's and Sotheby's always need their luxurious salerooms in London and New York? For that matter, will Tesco and WalMart need their giant retail outlets, if online ordering of routine purchases becomes the norm?)

3. It raises immediate questions about how manufacturers approach production and inventory issues and the disposal of surplus stock.

➡ NEW ANSWERS TO STOCK QUESTIONS

As product life-cycles in the computer industry have become ever more condensed, the arrival of the Web and its auction sites has given PC manufacturers some useful extra flexibility in dealing with end-of-range stocks. No-one wants an overhang of old stock sitting around, possibly at marked-down prices, in key retail outlets, where it is bound to blunt the impact of a new product line. Some manufacturers have set up online factory clearance stores to address this problem, but several leading players are now making deals with sites such as Onsale to auction off end-of-range computers and peripherals, in order to clear the decks quickly.

The initial aim is to achieve appropriate 'market clearance prices', but the makers have discovered that this can be quite a profitable procedure all round. The buyers obviously feel they are getting a good deal, since they are naming their own prices, and odd bits and pieces such as network cards can sometimes go for as little as a tenth of list price. On the other hand, notebooks and PCs often reach 90 per cent or more of the previous shop price – and since they are shipped direct from the warehouse, without any retailer or wholesaler taking a cut and with only a small fee going to the online auctioneer, the manufacturer can sometimes make a far juicier margin on these clearances than they ever did on conventional full-price retail sales.

Chapter 6
Shop, shop till the prices drop

'Merchants have no country.'
(Thomas Jefferson, 1814)

➡ THE REVOLUTION STARTS IN THE BOOKSHOPS

The very first personal business transaction most people will knowingly carry out over the Internet is likely to be the purchase of a book or a music CD. Whether you look at people shopping on the Internet from home or from their desks at work makes little difference. Apart from the remarkable freebie e-mail greetings card supplier Blue Mountain Arts (*http://www.bluemountainarts.com*), the most popular shopping sites on the Web are places like Amazon .com's mighty virtual bookshop (*http://www.amazon.com*) and its august rival, Barnes & Noble (*http://www.barnesandnoble.com*), CD and video specialist Columbia House (*http://www.columbiahouse .com*) and CDnow! (*http://www.cdnow.com*).

Blue Mountain Arts is a special case, as it is offering a completely free service (animated and customisable e-mail 'cards' that you send to your friends and loved ones to celebrate such essential festivals as Brothers' and Sisters' Day). The online auction sites, such as eBay and Onsale, are right up there, too, near the top of the charts compiled by research companies such as Media Metrix of New York. But these sites have created their own distinctive (and very substantial) niche markets and tend to attract people who have already tiptoed onto the Web and experimented with a few minor purchases. Mainstream Web retailing, as it has taken shape through 1997 and 1998, has been led by the bookshops and music stores. They have found customers in their millions who are happy to buy online – and investors in their tens of thousands who are anxious to get a piece of the big, highly visible, publicly traded companies like Amazon.com, Music Boulevard (*http://www. musicblvd.com*) and CDnow.

The products they sell are ideal for persuading hesitant first-timers to cast aside their inhibitions and make their first e-buys. Books, like CDs, are the same everywhere and do not need to be touched, tasted, test-driven or checked over by a trained mechanic. They are subject to formal or covert price fixing in many markets and vary hugely in price from country to country. And there are simply so many of them that, despite the best efforts of firms like Foyles in London and Barnes & Noble in the big American cities, no bookshop can hold physical stocks to cover every customer's desires. The fact that Amazon.com and the Barnes & Noble Website – and the Internet Bookshop (*http://www.bookshop.co.uk*), Bookpages (*http://www.bookpages.co.uk*) and Waterstones (*http:// www.waterstones.co.uk*) sites in the UK – can give buyers access to millions of titles, help track down out-of-print volumes, provide instant links to reviews and summaries and sometimes offer heavily discounted prices means that buying books online can be a rewarding experience.

➡ SOUND REASONS FOR A RE-THINK

With compact discs, the situation is equally promising for retailers prepared to build national and international businesses on the Web and for individuals seeking clear-cut bargains. Many people in the UK have long had the feeling that they were paying too much for CDs, cassettes and, before that, vinyl LPs. But it was not until the recent investigation into compact disc prices by the British Government's Monopolies and Mergers Commission (MMC) that it was officially confirmed that UK consumers pay through the nose for these items.

The MMC found that American prices for identical CDs were substantially lower than those in Britain, which may explain the number of enthusiastic British customers visiting the CDnow, Music Boulevard, CD World (*http://www.cdworld.com*) and CD Universe (*http://www.cduniverse.com*) sites – and, since mid 1998, the CD tributary of Amazon.com. All these companies have recognised the opportunity the Web gives them to build businesses very fast in their home markets and to pick up substantial numbers of overseas customers at the same time, almost as a by-product of marketing their wares on the Internet.

By giving their customers the chance to read press articles and reviews of new recordings and old compilations, see CD cover designs and listen to music clips – if necessary, many times over – before making the decision to buy, they can give isolated customers anywhere in the world, from Greenland to the Antarctic, a level of service that is comparable to that found in the best music shops. It doesn't matter to the individual, nor to the retailer, if a buyer is CD Universe's only customer in Bahrain, Bielefeld or Basingstoke. Because the customer pays the shipping charges, he or she costs no more to service than a CD buyer in nearby Boston.

➡ CD SAVINGS

How much difference in price is there for these worldwide commodities, selling in worldwide markets? The brutal answer is: quite a lot – and probably a good deal more than any record company or retailer can really justify.

Let's take one specific example: Eric Clapton's *Pilgrim*. This CD, priced at £16 in the UK, is listed at $12.47 from one of the leading online specialists. At the time of writing, that equates to about £7.56. In other words, the British price is more than double the American price. It's true that a buyer in the UK will have to think about adding shipping and handling costs on top of that, but all the online retailers will offer you a choice of despatch methods, with prices that depend on how fast you want your CD sent. All-in shipping and handling charges usually start at about $6 for one CD and another $1.50 for each subsequent item, for a fairly relaxed five-to-ten-day airmail delivery schedule. So the sums are quite straightforward. If you buy the Clapton CD online, you will have it in your hand, a week or so later, for a total cost of £11.20, rather than £16. It is completely legal and it's even rather good fun, buying CDs like this.

For those who can't wait – or, more probably, those who have almost left the birthday buying too late and need to be helped out of the mire – overnight transatlantic deliveries cost about $24 for one disc and $2.50 for each extra CD. That is getting quite expensive, but bear in mind that these outlets can offer you access to all kinds of obscure deletions, imports and rarities that might have taken months to track down in the old days. With a range of perhaps 200,000 discs to choose from at each of these sites, most people could think of something curious or nostalgic that would make an unexpected present for a valued friend. It is certainly true that the plain vanilla airmail option, coupled with the normal discounts available at these sites, is still likely to make the total cost of a new CD from CDnow or one of its rivals lower than the over-the-counter price for the same item at Our Price, HMV or Virgin in the UK.

http://www.cdnow.com
Eagle-Eye Cherry's CD is 40% cheaper online than in UK shops. Hear what it's like before you buy and get ideas about other albums you'd enjoy

➡ KNOW THE RULES AND AVOID THE PROBLEMS

What has held back much of the potential growth in Internet-based international retailing is people's fear of falling foul of customs and VAT regulations and finding that their bargain-hunting exploits have a sting in the tail. To some extent, this fear is valid. The exemptions for small, low-value imports of goods into the UK for personal use are by no means generous, though the first thing to be clear about is that there is no customs duty to pay on books. As long as books in Britain also continue to be free of VAT, this means that you can use the online booksellers to your heart's content.

For anything else – apart from alcohol, tobacco and perfumes, which are all subject to VAT and import duty and excise duty at prohibitive levels and must therefore be avoided like the plague – the effective limit to avoid both duty and VAT is a value of £18. That is not much. But it is, for example, enough to let you order a couple of current and discounted CDs (two copies of Clapton's *Pilgrim*, maybe) or, perhaps, three Golden Oldies compilations, while still staying within what is allowed.

HM Customs & Excise is already a little jumpy about Web-based goods and services, as well as it might be, given that the Internet could rapidly transform world trade patterns to the point where a surging tide of small transactions across national boundaries made the job of the customs officer totally impossible. Perhaps unexpectedly, though, it does have its own Website (*http://www.hmce.gov.uk/notices/143.htm*), with formal statements of the rules, some guidance and the phone numbers of Customs & Excise Advice Centres where you can find out what the law says about importing your particular online find. Gifts, incidentally, have to have been sent by a private individual to another private person, unpaid, for personal or family use and should be 'of an occasional nature', which means to do with Christmas or a birthday or anniversary or something similar. As long as these conditions are fulfilled and the goods are properly declared (and bearing in mind that it's all more complicated if alcohol, tobacco or perfumes are involved), gifts escape duty and VAT up to a value of 45 euros (approximately £36).

The regulations mentioned above are those applying to goods

purchased from countries outside the European Union, for the simple reason that all the significant online retailers that have emerged so far and that readers in the UK are likely to use are either based in Britain or across the Atlantic. Within the EU, VAT or the equivalent is added onto the price of your goods in the country of origin (except on cars, boats and aircraft, which few of us are likely to be ordering online) and there are no customs duties to worry about.

➡ SAFE ENOUGH TO BE GETTING ON WITH

The other reservation that deters many people from shopping over the Internet is the present uncertainty about payment methods. Horror stories about Internet credit card fraud have circulated right from the beginning, though there is little evidence to back most of them up.

The Barclays online shopping mall, BarclaySquare (*http://www.barclaysquare.co.uk*), has been doing business since 1995 and has never yet seen an Internet-based card fraud. There has been the usual range of cases involving unauthorised use and stolen cards, but nothing that could be put down to the transmission of card details over the Net. The big Web retailers all claim that card fraud is not a problem, even using the relatively crude security systems built into today's sites. But it is clear, anyway, that the individual shopper probably doesn't have much to worry about.

If credit card details were being intercepted and abused on any substantial scale, we would soon be receiving circulars from our card companies, either urging us not to give our card numbers over the Internet or threatening us with having to bear the full burden of these risky transactions ourselves. Most card issuers are members of APACS (the Association for Payment Clearing Services) and subscribe to the APACS banking code. This means that once you report a card stolen or alert the issuer to false transactions on your account, you are no longer at risk. Anything else that's taken will be refunded, with interest, by the card company. But you will only ever be liable for a maximum of £50 towards the losses before you alert the issuing company – and that £50 will usually be waived, unless you appear to have been negligent in some way. Thus, assuming, of course, that there is no complicity on your part in the misuse of your card, you are very unlikely to be out of pocket. And, as people in the business keep remarking, your card details are probably more vulnerable to copying and abuse when you allow the waiter at your holiday retreat to take your card into the back room as you pay for your restaurant meal.

The lurid tales that do occasionally surface only go to prove the point. There was the story of the journalist, reported in the *Sunday Times*, who discovered £1000 missing from his Lloyds account because of a payment to a jewellery shop in Abu Dhabi, a country he had never visited. Luckily, he had used his Visa/debit card to make a withdrawal from a hole-in-the-wall machine in Britain on the same day and it was quickly accepted that he was not liable for any of the missing money. He had, however, bought some software over the Internet from a site in Israel a few days before and paid by card, so the finger of suspicion clearly pointed towards this purchase. But whether the card details were taken off the Internet or simply noted down by someone unscrupulous at the other end – as they could easily be, every time we give our card details over the phone – was never established.

The point is that plastic is never a very secure way of doing business, even in the physical world. It is a practical, knockabout, rough and ready, good-enough-for-jazz sort of payment system at the best of times, and one that depends on the broad assumption that most people are honest and will consent to play by the rules. With the payment systems used by most online retailers, your transactions enjoy a very reasonable degree of security, particularly now that secure servers, using the technology known as SSL, or secure socket layers, are commonplace.

You can see this for yourself if you go to a respectable retailing site such as Waterstones or CD Universe to do a bit of shopping. When you have chosen the items you want and you click on the 'Pay now' or 'Cashier' button, the secure server at the other end sets up an encrypted link, over which the payment details are transferred. Look near the bottom of your screen. Depending on your choice of browser, you will almost certainly find that it is signalling to you automatically that you are connected to a secure site with SSL. It does this by showing a picture of either a key (broken for a non-secure site, whole for a secure one) or a padlock (closed for a secure site) in one of the lower corners of your screen. If you were about to buy from a retail Website and noticed that it was not flagged as secure, it might be sensible to avoid sending your card details online. Most Internet shopping sites are realistic enough to recognise that some customers may not trust the system to keep their details private and offer the option of arranging your transaction online but giving the necessary credit card information by phone or fax. They know, however, that the chances of anything going wrong are minute now, and getting smaller all the time as the technology and security systems are improved. This is a continuous process and one that is always advancing on several fronts at once. Card companies such as Mastercard, Visa and American Express, for example, have supported the development of an approach called the Secure Electronic Transaction protocol (SET, for short), which uses electronic signatures and encryption technology to make Web-based trading as safe as anyone is ever likely to want for routine use. Where SSL just secures the link, SET identifies the card owner as well. But the credit card companies are finding it hard to persuade banks and merchants to stump up large amounts of money to solve a problem of public perception that may just go away of its own accord. The amount of business done through online shops is surging and there is a strong suspicion now that customers' earlier security fears were partly rationalisations of a more general fear of the unknown. Once someone has bought once over the Internet – perhaps led on by the obvious bargains available online in books, CDs and computers – there is far less resistance to using this channel a second time.

➡ WHERE'S THE MICROMONEY?

If paying by credit card is the standard way of buying small, medium and large items over the Internet, what are we going to do about the rest? Card transactions become grossly uneconomical below about £5. Yet there are things that people might very well want to buy on the Web that would be worth £2, or 20p, or 2p, or even 0.2p. You can't buy anything in the shops for 0.2p, simply because the transaction costs, overheads and the assistant's time would swallow up the whole payment and more. But on the Web, where operations can take place in cyberspace and can be effectively instant, costless and fully automated, some people are going to get very rich selling millions of tiny fifth-of-a-penny slugs of information to willing buyers.

Out in the physical world – and on the Web, too, so far – choices often have to be made about whether to charge too much for something, with the obvious deterrent effect on sales, or to give it away, because the value people would be willing to pay would not justify its own collection costs. But imagine, for example, if Microsoft wanted its main Website to be a modest revenue-earner, rather than just a cost.

The big Microsoft site claims 200 million hits a day mostly from people who are quite firmly motivated to collect the information the company gives them. Let's assume that, say, 10 per cent of these people were looking for technical support and that Microsoft decided to charge them a nominal 1p per page (and here, for the first time ever, the idea of a nominal charge starts to have real meaning). No-one would be deterred and deflected from the mission of finding the necessary technical support. But look at what this would mean to Microsoft. It would represent an extra £200,000 a day, £50 million a year or more, conjured out of thin air. OK, maybe that wouldn't mean much to Microsoft, but it would to almost any other business on the planet.

The potential of micropayments, for specialised online news and share price services, for legal advice sites, indeed for any sort of information or entertainment service that could either persuade a few thousand people to dip in several times a day or millions to visit once or twice a week, is enormous. All that's missing is the dream of every e-business guru, from MIT's Nicholas Negroponte downwards, a widely acceptable microcash system that allows tiny shots of information to be sold at no cost to the marketeer. The MIT Media Lab and many others have been working towards this goal, which Negroponte believes will have been achieved before the end of the Internet landmark year of 1999.

➡ **SELL YOUR SALAMI BY THE SLICE**

But if micropayments are indeed the Holy Grail of Internet business, they have been a long time coming and there have been several casualties on the way. Companies such as CyberCash, First Virtual, Millicent (part of Compaq) and DigiCash have all promised us the earth in terms of microcurrencies and, so far, have fallen rather a long way short of changing the world – indeed, First Virtual has now been virtually folded into CyberCash. The technical problems are still huge and so is the problem of persuading a critical mass of banks and merchants to align themselves with one particular micropayment system.

The great practical advantage of SSL is that it is safe enough and uses an existing payment medium, in the form of credit cards. But the idea of micropayments is so important to the potential for new trading models on the Internet that it would be foolish to dismiss it. The commentators who wrote microcash's obituary in mid-1998, declaring it had been seen off by SSL and 'consigned to the scrapheap of cyberhistory', were merely demonstrating that they'd missed the point, unless someone can come up with an economical way of letting credit cards handle payments of a penny or less.

Quite apart from the mechanisms that will eventually allow such minute automated micropayments over the Web, others are working on the problem of devising e-money that will work more like ordinary coins and notes. A couple of new 'small payments' systems are being tried out in the UK, notably by BT and a group of retailing and publishing partners. BT's Array system (see *http://www.btarray.bt.com*) works for payments from 10p upwards and has been in commercial trials with an initial group of a dozen online stores and service companies. Array does not take a payment in advance, but tracks the customer's spending until it reaches a pre-set limit and then charges that amount across to a conventional credit card account.

The most interesting aspect of this trial is the involvement of Which?, with the *Which? Tax Savings Guide*, the *Which? Car Guide* and the *Which? Guide to Country Pubs*, and Hemmington Scott, which provides a Web-based investor information service (known as Company REFS) that Array customers can now access on a pay-per-view basis. The information used to be issued only in book or

CD form, either four or twelve times a year, at a subscription cost of either £295 or £675 per annum. This meant that the data was often some weeks out of date and that it would only sell to strongly motivated customers who had a pressing need for detailed information on many different firms. Now, in a classically Net-based shift of emphasis, small chunks of highly topical information can be sold for small amounts to much larger numbers of potential customers.

Chapter 7

Do we need an intranet here?

'Time is the measure of business.'

(Francis Bacon, 1625)

➡ THE TOOL FOR TOTAL TEAMWORK

The Internet is growing at breakneck speed, with more users, more uses and more Websites every day. By the summer of 1998, traffic volumes on the Net were doubling every 90 days, delegates to an Internet service providers' conference in Hungary were told. Yet it is generally believed that intranets are growing even faster, as companies that hesitate to take the plunge on the Internet race to exploit its technological spin-offs.

Everyone can see how intranets – private Internet-style networks, using the basic building blocks of the Net, such as Web pages, browsers and e-mail – can be useful in a big corporation. Ford's worldwide intranet, for example, links together nearly 90,000 professional staff in dozens of different countries and contains a mountain of information that is estimated at the equivalent of 30,000 pages of hard copy. Its home page receives more than a million hits a month from employees, for whom the Ford intranet has quickly become a vital part of the working toolkit, rather than a mere information stockpile. According to KPMG's management consultants, two-thirds of Britain's large companies now have intranets. But how useful could an intranet be in a small firm, where people already work closely together and see each other all the time?

The list of potential uses is surprisingly long, from scheduling meetings and sharing sales contact records to recording product specifications and propagating best-practice approaches to problems ('How do we deal with urgent customers who can't wait for normal delivery times?' and 'Who'll deliver a good pizza when we're all working late?'). You can use the intranet for expenses forms, for organising training courses and for making definitive, up-to-the-minute price lists accessible to everyone. If your people didn't have e-mail facilities before, they will quickly come to appreciate the advantages that brings, too, even within a single workplace. Creating an intranet also offers the possibility of making detailed technical or customer knowledge available at short notice to people who don't normally work with this information. Publishing takes seconds and it costs virtually nothing to add a few more documents to an internal Website, making sure their existence is sensibly signposted, so that they can be found when needed. Once this has been done, the absence of one key person who is off sick or away on holiday – a traditional cause of temporary paralysis in most small firms – becomes far less of a problem.

Unlike all previous attempts at making internal computer networks work as all-round productivity tools, an intranet has the huge advantage of being fun to use. The no-nonsense point-and-click technology that has fuelled the unstoppable rise of the World Wide Web is inviting, responsive and produces encouraging results for very little effort. It is easy to find information and easy to publish it. In companies that are growing fast and in danger of losing the personal touch that comes from everybody knowing everyone else by name, each person can be given a simple Web page with a photograph, contact details, a few details about his or her role and perhaps a line or two contributed by the individual about interests, hobbies or outside activities.

Space on the intranet is effectively free, so departments and workgroups can have their own pages, to do what they like with and to keep people in touch with each other for work and leisure purposes. Classified advertisements, bus and train timetables, restaurant recommendations, numbers for cab and courier companies and even horoscopes can attract people to make regular, casual visits. This is important, because it breeds familiarity with the equipment and the site. Just as playing Tomb Raider has trained many people to a surprising level of dexterity in the skills required to make a computerised figure jump up to a high ledge without falling off, looking up predictions about Libra's love life can be useful training. Come the day you need to delve into obscure documentation on the intranet to find out which components were used in a discontinued product you have never set eyes on, your easy familiarity with the site will be a real advantage to you and the company.

➡ SETTING UP AN INTRANET FROM SCRATCH

Probably because the Internet itself seems to breed so many myths, there are plenty that have already sprung up around the idea of intranets. One of the first is that they are expensive to set up. They can be, of course, if you are talking about a big international company and you decide to go for all the gold-plated options. But they are not inherently costly at all.

As long as you have a network connecting your existing computers, you are already most of the way there. You will need a half-decent PC to act as a server, but you can get hold of your server software free of charge (there's a modest free server software package downloadable from Microsoft at *http://www.microsoft.com/ie/* as an accessory to Internet Explorer) and you can buy a good HTML editor, such as Drumbeat, which will allow you to write the pages without getting bogged down in the intricacies of tags and codes, for no more than £425 ($700) or so. Drumbeat comes from Elemental Software (*http://www.elementalsw.com*) and you can download it straight away on a 30-day free trial. If £425 is too much to spend at this early stage, you can make a start with the basic editing software available with the Microsoft Internet Explorer browser or even use the Notepad text editor that comes with Windows. Put these elements together, dish out free copies of Internet Explorer (downloaded from the usual site, *http://www.micro soft.com/ie/*) to all your users and your intranet is in business. If there's not a network already in place, it will only take a £20 plug-and-play network interface card for each machine and some suitable cable and connectors to link a handful of PCs together into a workable intranet that'll span a distance of up to about 100 metres.

All this may sound a bit ramshackle and unplanned, but this is how many small company intranets begin and they are none the worse for it. The first few months of using the intranet you've got will tell you a lot more about the intranet you want, while proving the point that any intranet is usually a great deal better than none. Once you've lived with your improvised first-generation intranet for a while, there will be plenty of people around with good ideas about what should be added or changed in version 2.

It is also worth mentioning that the performance of your new intranet is quite likely to come as a pleasant surprise, compared with experiences you may have had using dial-up access to the World Wide Web. If you are taking advantage of an existing local area network in the office, for example, you will find it offers much better capacity and access speeds than any dial-up connection. Standard, cheap Ethernet cabling gives several times the capacity of an ISDN line, let alone an ordinary telephone line. As a result, things will fizz and zip about with impressive speed, screens will load quickly and you will probably be able to pile on the graphics, animation and multimedia effects to your heart's content, using far more gimmickry and bandwidth than you would dare to allow yourself when planning your public Website.

While there may be security or other reasons to restrict world-wide Internet access to a select group of employees, everybody in your firm should be connected, unhesitatingly, to the intranet. Even those who are in jobs where there is not a computer on the desk should be made to feel that the intranet is a resource that means something to them. They should be given an explicit right to sit down at a PC and explore the intranet, so that they become familiar with the home page and the basic facilities on offer, and should be encouraged to contribute to the build-up of useful content. This benefits everybody, and it even means that people who were originally employed without any computing skills at all are led by curiosity to train themselves in the basics of point-and-click.

➡ MAKE THE INTRANET SOMETHING FOR EVERYONE

It's quite a challenge for you, or whoever is nominated as the intranet Webmaster (the person who keeps the Website up to date), to make sure that there is enough attractive and relevant material on your pages to keep people coming back voluntarily, rather than just when the demands of the job make it necessary. Many firms in the medium-sized category, with, say, 100 to 500 employees, have looked at the production and printing bills for their short-run company magazines or newsletters and killed off the paper versions, giving their journals a new lease of life on the intranet. This is all very well if the content is compelling enough to persuade people to take a look, but it can backfire badly. Competitions, cartoon strips, job opportunities, house and car advertisements and special deals for employees set up with travel or car hire firms are some of the levers that can be used to entice people to open up an online company newspaper. If they fail, however, it has to be acknowledged that the chairman's message or the production director's rousing appeals to everyone to try harder may fail to reach their targets. Unlike a newpaper, which may sit around on the corner of someone's desk for weeks and then be picked up and read, an intranet page that has no pulling power is likely to remain firmly closed. No one medium is suitable for every purpose, and the office noticeboard still has its place, even though many of the items pinned up there may also be found on the intranet.

Once a company has decided to make the intranet part of its way of working, it becomes vital that it is for everybody. One fast-growing business we know took the rather brutal step of junking all its internal telephone directories and lists overnight, so that the intranet suddenly became the only place to find a number. This caused some grumbles, but then so do printed directories, which quickly become out of date. At least with the new system updates can be carried out instantly and at no cost, as soon as changes occur, and whole lists don't have to be reprinted and reissued whenever a couple of people or departments swap jobs or move offices. Why not put the daily canteen menu on the intranet? At least it guarantees that a fair number of people will be prompted by their stomachs, some time in the latter half of the morning, to consider going online and seeing what's cooking.

Generally speaking, putting something up on the intranet will be quicker, cheaper and more flexible than immortalising it in print on paper. And how do you begin to quantify the real, practical business advantage of being able to get new information to the people who need it faster, right across the company? That is something that feeds through directly into the day-to-day performance of the whole workforce.

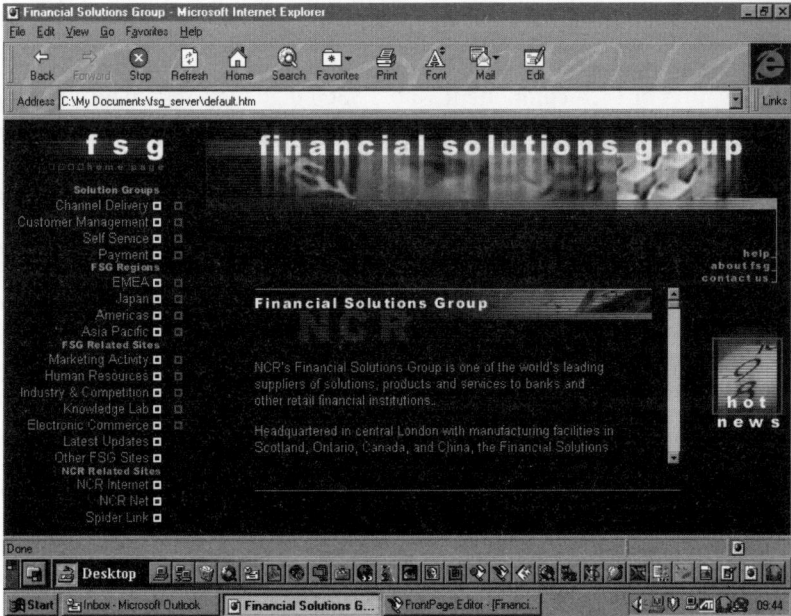

The intranet at work: NCR's Financial Solutions Group's site fosters teamwork by giving employees around the world a finger on the pulse

➡ A TOOL FOR TACKLING THE IMPOSSIBLE

Among the big international corporations, there are many that have taken to heart the new opportunities created by the arrival of intranets. They have used them as tools in radical business process re-engineering initiatives, changing the way work gets done and consigning mountains of manuals, rulebooks, memos and forms to the corporate bonfire.

When Motorola developed a new high-speed modem to link

people to the Internet via cable TV connections, it needed to bring it to market quickly. Production on the two new assembly lines at its factory in Massachusetts had to start within six weeks – and the engineers could see at a glance that the new product was going to be complex and hard to make. The deadline appeared impossibly tight. It would normally have taken months just to produce full assembly instructions and engineering drawings. Instead, Motorola scrapped all that, took a large number of high-resolution pictures of each component with a $500 digital camera, rigged up an intranet and published the images and instructions online.

There was already a computer network at the plant, which allowed Motorola to put the intranet in place cheaply, for less than $5000. But no-one had ever worked this way before, without technical drawings, and most of the intranet's users had never had any contact with the Web, so the company was taking a real chance on the new methods. It had a hot new product and a chance to win a share of an important new market, but any delays or quality lapses could have had expensive consequences. In the event, though, the initiative was triumphantly successful. Production started on time, quality was good and the new way of working proved measurably cheaper. Where each pair of assembly lines would normally have needed three support technicians just to manage the documentation, Motorola found the two cable modem lines could be looked after by just one person.

➡ THE INTRANET AS A WAY OF WORKING

The creation of Ford's giant intranet was a very different operation – not an improvised response to a sudden need but a deliberate and carefully planned policy initiative with one declared aim: 'To move to the Ford intranet as our way of doing business.' For the world's fourth-largest industrial company to talk in those terms, something big has to be happening.

So what do Ford's 90,000 intranet users get out of it? They get almost all the answers they would have had to chase up on the phone or look up in libraries and archives, classified under several broad headings on the home page (known as the Ford Hub): news, people, processes, products and competition. Each of these categories then fans out to cover a wealth of information. Competition, for example, delves into areas such as benchmarking, motor shows, global market information, competitor news, product-cycle plans and patent information.

People can also access phone books, training registration forms, maps, building layout details, human resources information and feeds from the Ford Communications Network, the internal CCTV channel. Individuals can locate the information that empowers them to do more and do it better. Product teams can examine detailed pictures from 'teardowns', where competitors' vehicles are dismantled and dissected, scan through the minutes of past problem-solving meetings and learn from the candid comments recorded in other Ford teams' TGW ('things gone right/wrong') files. And the company? Its corporate goals of 'better quality, better speed, better cost' have been served in dozens of different ways. 'This is the best thing we've ever seen for capturing knowledge, knowing who's doing what, cutting information and distributing it in different ways,' says one of Ford's top executives.

There are fewer mistakes – and fewer excuses. 'Everything goes on the Web,' says one project manager, part of a Taurus/Sable team that includes hundreds of engineers, scattered over several countries. 'The Web is the master copy and everyone's on the same page. We no longer get people coming out of the woodwork at the eleventh hour and claiming they didn't receive the latest information.'

While Ford's notorious document store at an old factory in Michigan admits that it can sometimes take its researchers six months to find a particular piece of paper in the 15-foot-high stacks of cardboard boxes, the intranet may have saved the car maker from drowning in a sea of paper. One of the triggers for the development of the internal Web was a set of in-house surveys that asked white-collar workers at Ford whether they had access to the information they needed to do their jobs properly. A fraction over half said yes. The rest – some 40,000 well-paid, well-educated professionals and managers around the world – said they didn't, so they couldn't. If Ford hadn't discovered the virtues of the intranet in the nick of time, it might well have been on its way to becoming a fatally unmanageable business.

➡ THE CHICKEN OR THE EGG?

For Ford, the mighty intranet came a year or so after the establishment of the company's main external Website. In fact, one of the ways the intranet team supported its arguments involved pointing to a Ford vehicle development team that was already using the Web, very successfully, to collaborate on research, design and engineering. For many small firms, however, the intranet may come first, before there is any question of opening up to the big, wide world of the Internet.

In practice, this can work out well. You stumble around and make any mistakes that are going to happen, without having to worry about the glare of publicity, the danger of confusing your established customers or the attentions of hackers or competitors. While you are not hooked up to the outside world, no-one can hack in. And when you do decide that at least some of your employees should be able to chase information across the World Wide Web, there are some fairly tough, cheap weapons available to ward off unwanted strangers. These include firewalls (software filters that bar outsiders from accessing your server), password authentication systems and post-dial codes that can fool intruders even when they think they've skipped over the hurdles and got inside your system. At this point too, once the appropriate security measures are in place, you can make dial-up access to the intranet available, so that your people can log in and pick up the information they need while they are out on the road.

➡ REACHING OUT TO YOUR BRANCHES

If you operate from several offices, or have a service network with scattered individuals or branches, the benefits of setting up an intranet can be even more marked. It's not just a question of having to send fewer bulky manuals and reference documents out around the country and cutting down on the number of long-winded and unproductive phone calls. The impact is more widespread, with positive effects on morale, performance and costs at many different levels.

If your company's branches are already linked on a computer

network, bringing the intranet to the regions is not going to be a problem. But there are two or three different ways to approach it if you are a smaller and less well-equipped company – and they do not necessarily involve any great costs or complexity.

One route is to settle for the kind of dial-up access mentioned above, where a security code number is demanded after the ordinary telephone number. A more satisfactory approach is to place the whole intranet behind a reasonably secure firewall – which you will soon want to do anyway, as the Web becomes an irresistible magnet for business activity – and establish that only traffic from certain specified Internet addresses (confirmed by the use of digital ID certificates) is to be allowed in through the wall. These addresses, of course, are those of your branches, which will then be free to access whatever material they need, whenever they need it. The third option is to set your whole intranet up as a public Internet site and depend solely on password protection systems for the security of those documents that must not be seen by the outside world. This is getting into the realms of fairly flimsy security, but it may be the most suitable interim solution for a small firm that is not staking its all on the success of the intranet and is prepared to be selective about what is put up on its site.

The advantages of connecting branch offices up to an intranet become apparent very quickly. Instead of feeling isolated, people in the far-flung outposts can be sure they are always working from the same up-to-date prices, customer lists and specifications as those at head office. Suddenly, their quoted delivery dates are informed by the ability to check stock and spares availability online and place orders immediately – all without descending into the primitive world of faxes, answering machine messages and multi-coloured four-part form sets. Recurrent problems can be looked up in files modelled on the World Wide Web's familiar FAQ (frequently asked questions) pages, with photographs and diagrams as required, while really awkward queries can be e-mailed off instantly to the appropriate technical or business experts, for informed analysis and comment. Both the feelings and the reality of teamwork are enhanced, because this cheap, flexible technology means people are genuinely able to work more closely as a team, adapting more responsively to each others' needs.

➡ DON'T LET THE NETS START BREEDING

The creation of an intranet will remove barriers and foster a much stronger sense of collaboration across almost any geographically dispersed organisation, whether it is linking 18 people or 80,000.

It is a good idea, though, to ensure that it remains as one company-wide intranet, with some co-ordinating guidance to keep tabs on who publishes what. Completely separate intranets for individual offices or departments have worked well enough in some large and medium-sized firms, but experience has indicated that there are definite pitfalls to watch out for.

Branch or departmental intranets can be a stimulating outlet for the ideas and creativity latent in the workforce, but they can also spin off out of control. It's good to encourage enterprise and free expression. It's not so good to generate uncertainty and confusion. If too many people are publishing different company documents on their branch or departmental intranets, there are bound to be problems sooner or later – probably when someone innocently takes an out-of-date version as gospel and only finds out too late that company policy has changed.

➡ WHAT COULD WE DO WITH AN INTRANET THAT WE COULDN'T DO BEFORE?

There will be exceptions in specific industries and situations, but, despite Motorola's success in meeting an outrageously tight production deadline, having an intranet won't usually make it possible to do things that were impossible before. What it will do is enable you to get all sorts of things done a great deal faster and more cheaply, just as the train, the telephone and the fax all had the effect of speeding up the pace of business life when they arrived on the scene.

This acceleration factor makes itself felt at many different levels, but it is often seen at its most clear-cut in relation to the kind of banal business housekeeping activities that can leave us feeling thwarted and exhausted before we have even started doing anything that might reasonably be classed as work. Let's look at a typical process for ordering a box of standard ballpoint pens from a large organisation's central stores, before and after the coming of the company's intranet:

Before the intranet	After the intranet
Spend ten minutes looking for order form	Call up order form on intranet from page stored in 'favourites' or 'bookmarks' list
Spend five minutes looking for ballpoint pen	Check appropriate boxes and select cost code from drop-down table
And another three for one that works	Press 'send' button
Fill in form, in triplicate	
Call colleague for reminder of cost code	
Find and use Tipp-Ex to correct errors	
Separate copies. Keep one and send one to finance and one to stores in internal post	
Messenger's wife is sick. He's gone home, so no mail collection till Monday	
Return voicemail message from clerk in stores who can't decipher your writing	
Pens delivered	Pens delivered

This may seem a trivial example – but that's just the point. We could all fly high, think great thoughts and be capable of great things if we didn't get bogged down in the trivial, the circumstantial and the routine. The ability to win back time and energy from the trivial for use on the important issues is a major consequence of improved ways of working. Even in a small firm with 10 or 12 people, saving less than an hour of productive time per person per day is the equivalent of having an extra member of staff – and that extra person is not some trainee from the Jobcentre who knows nothing about your business, because the time you are saving is that of the experienced and knowledgeable people who already run the firm. If the intranet can make these mundane procedures and activities less distracting, it is doing a good job, even before you start to factor in the more dramatic improvements it can bring in its wake.

➡ IF WE SET UP OUR WEBSITE ON THE INTERNET, CAN'T WE USE THAT INSTEAD OF AN INTRANET?

The major benefits you get from an intranet often stem directly from the fact that it carries live, private, no-holds-barred information to help your people work better together. Any good intranet is stuffed with commercially sensitive material, subjective assessments of customers, competitors and suppliers that might well be libellous if published outside, ridiculous in-jokes and bits and pieces of domestic trivia. None of this would be appropriate on the Website, where the company's products, strengths and brand values need to be put across brightly and purposefully to strangers and potential customers. A certain gloss is necessary, quite out of keeping with the boots-and-all energy and robust sense of community fostered by the intranet.

An intranet needs to give real value to your people. A Website needs to give real value to your customers. Because their needs are so different, the two should be kept carefully segregated, even when you get to the stage of having links in and out, through the firewall, from your intranet to the Internet world outside.

In many ways, what you find on a company's intranet is what

the company is really like. Knowing what was published in all the nooks and crannies of your competitors' intranets would certainly tell you a great deal about their plans, morale and attitudes. But that works in reverse, too, and it has to be admitted that the existence of a lively, well-used intranet does raise some security implications for your company. Parts of the site can be guarded by password systems. Other items can be tucked away out of sight without necessarily invoking any formal security procedures.

One executive we know claims the key to reasonable, practical security within the intranet is simply to pay close and careful attention to the naming of files and the wording of hot-linked phrases: 'If you dub something "red faces" or "customer gossip" or "Project Bastille", you are going to have hundreds of hits a week on it – and quite right, too,' she says. 'If I have anything I want to put on the intranet but keep within a fairly small circle, I choose a label like "quality matrix" or "standards proposal (rejected draft)". That guarantees no-one will go there, at least on purpose. Who needs passwords or encryption, when you've got TQM jargon to protect your files?'

Chapter 8
From extranet to ultranet

'To get others to come into our ways of thinking, we must go over to theirs.'

(William Hazlitt, 1850)

➡ DO WE WANT OUR SUPPLIERS ONLINE WITH US?

If you try to imagine something halfway between your public Internet site and your private, employees-only intranet, you arrive at a curious beast known as an extranet.

Extranets are a hot topic at the moment, because they are suddenly allowing large corporations to work far more closely with their customers, distributors and suppliers than ever before. For years, they have talked big about just-in-time delivery and manufacturing processes and tried to make them happen by cobbling together computer networks based on proprietary software and customised applications that were expensive to build and a pain to support. Suddenly, the Internet has provided the common technical platform to simplify and speed up all these projects, with the added bonus that the Web's friendly, unthreatening point-and-click interfaces make sophisticated systems easy for anyone to use.

The idea is that an extranet connects your key business partners directly to the relevant bits of your intranet, so that they can collect information and even perform approved actions without having to involve your staff. Boeing has already opened up 75 extranets, linking it with the airlines, its contractors and various US Government agencies. Hewlett Packard and Procter & Gamble have set up extranets reaching out to their advertising and marketing agencies. General Electric has built a whole extranet marketplace it calls the Trading Process Network, within which 2000 suppliers and a dozen large buyers jostle for contracts. Through the TPN extranet, GE places $1 billion-worth of orders a year and saves itself an estimated $160 million per annum. Adaptec, which makes computer storage devices, has spent $1 million on a long-distance extranet to tie it more closely to its Taiwanese chip suppliers, halving chip delivery times, saving $1 million a year in direct costs and pruning a vital $9 million from the cost of its work-in-progress pipeline. If all these big American companies are falling over themselves to exploit the potential of extranets, shouldn't smaller firms in the USA and the rest of the world be rushing to build them too?

➡ AN EXTRANET OF OUR OWN?

On the whole, small firms are remarkably resistant to business fads and fashions. It's one of the strengths that helps the better ones survive. And there will be few people in smaller companies, particularly in the UK, who really feel that a sudden surge of interest in extranets among large US corporations necessarily points to anything much more than the arrival of another flavour of the month. That's laudable scepticism. But it shouldn't obscure the fact that many small to medium businesses have plenty to gain from being aware of extranets as a potentially useful and affordable tool in their armoury.

So why might your company think about setting up an extranet? For a start, there's often lots of information on an intranet that you'd like your trusted suppliers and customers to have access to but that you might not want the general public to see – phone lists, ordering procedures, distributor agreements and so on. You can't dump these details out onto the Website for public consumption. But you may well draw the line at inviting even your trusted business partners into the full intimacy of your intranet. How you do it is up to you. You may well choose to set up the extranet as a separate physical entity, if only to make security less of an issue, but you can then simply copy these files over from your intranet server to their home on the extranet.

Then you can begin to build onto this the stuff that really makes an extranet special, the information that can be shared to ease the flow of commerce to and from your partners upstream and downstream. This will tend to be dynamic data, relating to generic questions like stock levels, production plans, price changes and orders and to the specific needs of your particular business.

If there are particular information bottlenecks that routinely cause problems for you and your business partners, it is well worth looking at them again to see if an extranet might provide an unexpected solution. This may sound a bit like the classic 'To the man with a hammer, every problem looks like a nail'. But this is a new hammer, the idea of which did not enter into anyone's calculations even three or four years ago – and information, in this context, could take many different forms, not necessarily to do with numbers and prices.

It makes good sense to re-examine old problems in the light of new and affordable technologies. One American winemaker, for example, wanted to raise the quality of the grapes it bought in from independent growers – which hardly sounds, on the face of it, like an information problem. But the company already paid out for high-definition satellite photographs from NASA, which it used to identify disease and other problems in its own vineyards. Realising that its pictures also showed other vineyards in the area, it decided to set up an extranet link to each of its regular independent suppliers so that the satellite images could be used by them, too, to monitor crops and nip problems in the bud. The result is a three-fold improvement: better grapes, better wine and better business relationships.

➡ THE DAY ROVER TURNED ON A SIXPENCE

In Britain, there has generally been a tendency to lag a step or two behind America in the adoption of the techniques and technologies made available by the Internet. But there are some impressive examples of what can be done in the UK, once a company spots an opportunity and gets the bit between its teeth – and the businesses involved are not always those with a reputation for being fast on their feet.

Rover Group entered the mid-1990s with grandiose plans for a heavyweight, state-of-the-art, multi-million-pound internal network to link its car factories, warehouses and offices. Development work had been going on for many months and the first roll-out sites had already been lined up, when a few far-sighted individuals in the group's information technology department suddenly realised they were on the wrong track. To Rover's credit, the investment it had already sunk into the big project was quickly written off and the plans were totally redrawn, to give the car maker a huge, flexible intranet instead, based on cheap and standardised Internet technologies and point-and-click Web browsers.

Like the Ford intranet, Rover's internal Web became the first computing and communications system to have a transforming effect on the way people across the company worked and interworked with each other. Unlike Ford, though, Rover moved quickly on to extend the principle to include its distribution outlets in Britain and Europe. Plans were soon in place for a series of extranets, reaching out to connect 650 UK dealers and some 600 distributors in several European countries.

Though the dealerships are independent businesses, rather than Rover subsidiaries, they are given access, through the extranet, to a vast amount of commerically sensitive information about model availability, spares, delivery dates and policy and marketing initiatives. Access is restricted to certain parts of the Rover intranet by a system of passwords and firewalls, but the dealers are trusted with a far more privileged and comprehensive view of what goes on inside Rover than ever before. As a result, they are more in tune with the company's thinking, more successful at selling the cars, more inclined to feed back detailed information from the front line, where people's opinions of new models are sometimes expressed with admirable frankness, and less likely to desert the Rover franchise for the chance to offer Japanese or Korean vehicles.

Even with over 1200 distribution points to be connected, the extranets presented surprisingly few technical problems. Cross-platform compatibility – the ability to work with many different types of computer and operating systems – is one of the less obvious virtues of the Web technologies. But it enables intranets and extranets to sidestep a morass of integration issues and Rover took full advantage of it to bring its international army of independently minded business partners on board in double-quick time.

➡ BORN TO BE FILED

One of the important advantages of a well-thought-out extranet is the fact that there are usually fairly substantial advantages for the business partners on the outer periphery, as well as the company at the centre of things. People who don't like being pushed around to suit someone else's convenience can often be led to co-operate willingly, if they can see what's in it for them.

Legendary American motorcycle manufacturer Harley-Davidson has created an extranet linking the company to over 400 dealers, making life easier for everyone by allowing them to submit warranty claims directly into its systems, instead of indirectly via forms, faxes, letters and phone calls. Dealers who used to have to fill in a printed form with lengthy vehicle identification numbers and parts codes always suspected that some of the delays in paying their claims came about simply because of misreading or miskeying of the codes at the other end. They were right, of course, because mistakes are inevitable in manual systems like that.

Now there is no rekeying and the dealers receive their warranty payments in 48 hours, rather than four or five weeks. And that's just the start. Already, dealers can take advantage of a 24-hour, seven-day-a-week service that lets them put in financial statements and requests for technical documentation, download exploded-view diagrams of engines and gearboxes and check for product recall information. Soon, they will be able to order Harley-Davidson spares and accessories from the Web-type pages, even if the dealership computer systems they use are not directly compatible with the ones at Harley's offices. In a few years' time, when sending video pictures across the Net is cheap and easy, a dealer on the West Coast with an Electra Glide that's playing up will be able to show it live and close up, with full sound effects, to the technical staff at the company's headquarters in Milwaukee for an expert diagnosis.

➡ HOW EVOLUTION GAVE FEDEX AN ULTRANET

http://www.fedex.com
Federal Express employees jumped the counter and used the Web-based
parcel tracking interface originally intended for FedEx customers

Sometimes what happens in the real world isn't exactly what the
planners had in mind. It is quite possible to end up with out-and-
out hybrids that are, strictly speaking, neither intranet or extranet.
That is what has evolved at Federal Express, where the Net-based
approach to getting things done has taken on a life of its own.

It all started with the simple proposition that customers should
be able to check up for themselves on the progress of their parcels

and packages through the worldwide FedEx distribution system. This was clearly what they wanted and the company recognised that it would also lighten the load on FedEx staff charged with answering enquiries and progress chasing parcels to keep the customer satisfied.

A public Website was set up, with a straightforward interface to the main FedEx tracking system, and customers were invited to log in at any time, give their customer number and the identifying details for a particular parcel and see for themselves how far it had got. It was an extra service element for those customers who wanted it, but anyone who did not like the idea of DIY tracking could just pick up the phone and get a FedEx employee to trace the package by logging into a computer and using the long-established bar-code tracking system (set up in the early 1980s, incidentally, by the man who became Netscape's CEO, Jim Barksdale).

Once the new, fast and friendly Web interface was in place, however, few staff members chose to use the 'official' route into the system. They found it easier to jump the counter and pretend to be customers and they made their preference felt so emphatically that it provoked a major rethink. Federal Express now has a full-blown intranet, the Internet Website and extranets out to several of its major trading partners, all so intertwined and cross-linked that it is hard to tell where one ends and the other begins. This kind of all-embracing 'ultranet' is probably the logical conclusion for many companies, as they develop more and more of their business processes and relationships in ways that stem directly from the experience of using Web technologies.

Chapter 9
Internet business is still about business

'Only connect!'

(E. M. Forster,1910)

➡ COULD WE DO IT? SHOULD WE DO IT?

If you are starting to develop your own ideas about how the Web can be used to boost your business, you may already be beginning to wonder about the practicalities, costs and pitfalls of designing and building a Website. This is an area where you will not be alone for long. As soon as people get a sniff of the fact that there is a new project in the air, designers and Web experts of every persuasion will come flocking to give you the benefit of their advice, followed, they hope, by their invoices. It is a fact of life that not all this advice will be the well-meaning, dispassionate, disinterested guidance it purports to be. The next two chapters are aimed at giving you the knowledge and arming you with the right questions to spike a few guns and cut through a lot of the clutter as you try to settle the three key issues:

- What is the Website for?
- Where will it be?
- Who will design and build it?

As soon as you start thinking about launching a site and putting your own material on the Web, you face the question of where you are going to rent commercial site space on a Web server. Your Internet service provider will probably be your first port of call and may be able to offer you a very good deal. You need some basis for comparison, though, so it may also be worth talking to a specialised Web-hosting service, such as BT WebWorld or the highly rated Virtual Internet.

BT WebWorld, obviously aware that it is likely to be seen as a safe bet by nervous newcomers, offers two all-in start-up packages that include site design, registration of your unique address on the Web (known as your 'domain name') and Web hosting. The Easy Start package costs £725 for a very basic site with four pages, four graphics and 200 words of text, plus an online form, if required, with 10 Mb of storage, a maximum of 100 Mb of traffic per month and a Web address in the form *http://www.yourname.com* or *co.uk*. The Custom Start deal offers a bigger site with up to 30 scanned images, design and marketing consultancy help and options such as SSL (Secure Socket Layer encryption for credit card payments) and password-controlled closed user groups. At £1700, this is not necessarily a cheap way to make a start on the Web, though BT does sometimes run cut-price offers to drum up business. There are also pure hosting services from £20 a month.

The normal commercial package offered by other Web hosts includes a rather larger amount of space (perhaps 20 Mb or 25 Mb) on a high-performance server, with direct, dedicated, high-capacity private circuit links to the Internet. The fixed charge of £100 to £200 a year for this space will cover a certain number of hits per month, expressed in terms of, say, 500 Mb per month of data transfer. This can be confusing. Each hit does not represent a visitor, let alone a customer arriving at your site, because a hit is only a request for an individual document or file (it could even be just a single illustration, on a page where half a dozen were used). One interested visitor may well chalk up 10, 15 or even 20 or more hits in the course of exploring your pages. Nevertheless, these data transfer limits are usually pitched at a fairly generous level, so it would take a very big, busy – and, hence, successful – site to incur extra charges. Virtual Internet, for example, says that its monthly data transfer threshold is exceeded by fewer than one in 50 of its customers, as 500 Mb is enough to support many thousands of hits. If your newly established site attracted contacts and enquiries at such a rate, you would no doubt be delighted to shell out a small bonus to your Web host, especially since such an arrangement would give you the capacity to move smoothly up to handle even higher response levels. Compared with the capital investment, technical demands and revenue costs of owning, accommodating, maintaining and administering a powerful Web server on your own premises, these hosting services can provide excellent value for money.

➡ HAND IT OVER OR GO IT ALONE

The other popular approach to launching your company and products out onto the Web is to hand over all the technical service and support aspects of the operation to the consultants or designers who have planned and built your Website for you. These people will be used to offering a full package of services to their clients and will either set up your pages on their own servers or arrange a deal with a Web hosting specialist. They will also handle the essential housekeeping tasks for you, such as the registration of your domain name, announcements to the appropriate search engines and directories and the maintenance and updating of your pages. If secure processing facilities are needed, so that payment information and credit card numbers can be transmitted in encrypted form, they will make arrangements for an appropriate level of security.

The final option – and it is a bold step to take, unless you can be very sure about how far and fast your business on the Web is going to grow – is the full-blown do-it-yourself approach. For some new sites – where, for example, a software start-up company is making its debut and the whole business is intended to revolve around the Internet marketplace – it is the natural choice. If the right technical sophistication and experience are available in-house, it may make sense for a company to take the plunge straight away and opt to maintain complete control by hosting its own site on its own server. Generally speaking, however, for companies that operate in the physical world as well, hosting your own site is not the best way to start out on the process of tapping the Internet's potential. It is usually more productive to farm out the technical aspects of setting up and running your site and concentrate on the absolute business essentials – what your Website will do and how it will attract and satisfy the people you want to reach.

➡ WHAT SHOULD YOUR SITE BE LIKE?

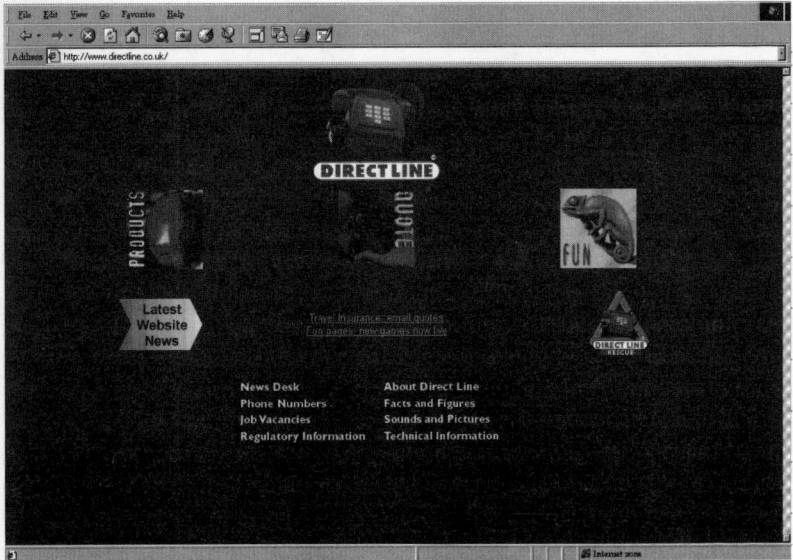

http://www.directline.co.uk
Direct appeal: a no-nonsense, businesslike site from an insurer that has already transformed its industry once by exploiting new marketing channels

The key factor in any site's success is how it makes the user feel. You're a user. Click into some of the interesting sites recommended in Chapter 12 and see how they make you feel. Do they seem quick and responsive? Do they look interesting? Have they anticipated the subjects you want to know about and the questions you want answered? Do they inspire confidence? If you know the companies involved, does the image that comes across from the Website match the image formed from your previous contacts with the company and its products, services and advertising?

You are not alone. Whatever your reactions are, many other people, viewing the same Website, will react with the same delight, interest, indifference or disappointment. What works for you will usually work for others. What annoys or irritates you will infuriate people who place a very high value on their time. If you click out of a commercial site feeling that it was probably designed by 20-year-olds with 14-year-olds in mind, it is the site that has got it wrong, not you. If your reaction is that the designers have not taken the trouble to give you what you want from the site, you are right, more or less by definition. When it comes to briefing the specialists to develop your own Website, tell them as much as you can about what impressed and what dismayed you in your sampling of other people's sites.

Make a note of which sites drew you in and encouraged you to stay and explore. Notice how certain sites tail off abruptly the moment you move beyond the home page, making it a bit too clear that all the money, all the creativity and all the effort have been invested there. At the same time, notice how offputting an unashamedly frothy, gimmicky home page can be, especially if it is supposed to be inviting you to do serious business. There are compromises to be struck in Website development, as in all other forms of marketing communication, and pitching the tone correctly for the business concerned is a matter of sensitivity and fine tuning.

➡ WHAT THEY SEE IS WHAT YOU ARE

For over a hundred years, salesmen have been trotting out the old adage that you never get a second chance to make a first impression. In this new world of electronic business, it is as true as ever. As the home page of your Website materialises before your potential customer's eyes, you have a maximum of two minutes to make an impact.

You are addressing this person through a tiny window into his or her world, probably measuring no more than 12″ by 9″ (the PC screen may call itself a 15″ model, but remember that's the diagonal measurement). All the carefully nurtured brand values implicit in your advertising, packaging, arts sponsorship and product design seem a long way off in this context. It is only what you give your Website visitors on the screen that is going to carry your brand values through into cyberspace. What they see is what you are. And that gives rise to both problems and opportunities.

The opportunities are fairly obvious. If you can strike the right note and make the right offer, you can generate completely new business from scratch, even from customers who would never previously have come across your company. In some commodity-type sectors, such as books, music, office supplies, travel or branded clothing, you can certainly hope to clinch sales over the Internet as the result of your very first contact with a customer. If the product does not need to be touched and tasted and you can reassure visitors to your site about privacy, data and financial security and your own commercial probity, the chance of making a direct and virtually costless sale is always there.

The problems are sometimes less apparent. You may have real and meaningful brand values and an established corporate reputation within the geographical or business community you tradition-ally trade in. But the outsider who comes to you via the Web may know nothing of these. Your advertising may have been a mainstay of the trade papers in your area for many years and you may have appeared at countless shows, conferences and exhibi-tions, but this could mean nothing at all to a newcomer from a different industry sector or a different country or region.

Your first reaction may be to think that no-one who doesn't already know you could ever be interested in what you have to sell. But if there's one thing the short and tumultuous history of the Web demonstrates, it's the fact that the most interesting and dramatic deals often come from the most unexpected quarters. It is not just the ability to create almost frictionless markets that matter. The Web has also brought us much nearer to a frictionless flow of ideas, not least because visionaries who have just conceived zany, off-the-wall business ideas that they would not want to expose to the glare of other people's ridicule can now begin to follow them up, quickly, cheaply and unobtrusively, without drawing attention to their information-gathering activities.

➡ HOW NOT TO DO IT

As is often the case, one of the easiest ways of learning how to do things right is to look at how other people contrive to get them so badly wrong. Here are some of the classic pitfalls that must be avoided if your Website is to make a positive impact and do the job it sets out to do.

Graphics too big

Make your graphics large and complicated enough and your pictures too big and you can guarantee your site will take so long to download, even with a reasonably fast modem, that people will become irritated and frustrated while waiting for your home page to appear.

Dead-end streets

Far too many sites fail to make it obvious how people can obtain further information about the product or service or the company. We have seen some that do not include even a phone or fax number or an e-mail address, let alone the online enquiry, registration or order forms potential customers might hope to find.

Bad housekeeping

Sites that advertise the owner's lack of attention to detail with glaringly misspelt words do not inspire confidence. Nor do broken hypertext links that lead to nowhere or to an 'under construction' sign. Tags that say 'Last updated November 98' give hostages to fortune – if the site is not going to be kept bang up to date, it should not draw attention to its inadequacies.

Shrines to the corporate ego

If you wanted a complete history of the company, with in-depth profiles of each of its directors, or a detailed description of each of its office properties and manufacturing facilities, wouldn't you phone the press and PR people and get it sent to you on paper? The Web is not usually the place for exhaustive background material. Many sites are cluttered with this stuff, but it's usually there because the site designers are busy toadying to the worst instincts of senior managers.

Dumping grounds for unwanted information

Does the site need to carry versions of every sales brochure? It may sometimes have an important role as a repository of technical advice and information for a specialist audience, but the main purpose of almost every site – and certainly the home page – is to develop a relationship with an audience and establish brand values.

Poor signposting

If people can't make their way around quickly and intuitively and find what they want, they won't stay. Poor navigation costs customers. A vital saving grace is often the provision of plenty of clearly highlighted opportunities to skip back to the home page and start again.

Leaps in the dark

It takes time to download pages and scan them to see if they offer what you want. Links that invite you to click on a phrase or a picture but don't make it at all clear what to expect are frustrating. They waste time and get in the way of the fulfilment of your mission, leaving you quite entitled to feel that the site has not been planned with much consideration for your convenience.

➡ GROUND RULES FOR SUPER SITES

The temptation is to look at a list of banana skins like this and think that as long as they are all sidestepped, your own site will turn out all right. Unfortunately, it's not quite as simple as that. The sins outlined above are major mistakes, the sort of thing that causes credibility to haemorrhage away. But merely avoiding such howlers does not guarantee an attractive and effective Website.

Good sites leave you feeling the visit was worth it

Surfing is on the wane. People aren't interested in wandering aimlessly around the Web now, for the pleasure of seeing what they happen to stumble across. It's too big, and too slow, for that to be much fun. They visit sites because they want to do something – track down information, talk to you or buy a product or service. If you frustrate their intentions with a badly planned and designed site, they have a worldwide selection of alternative sources to choose from and they will go elsewhere without a second glance.

If the visitor to your site is likely to be wanting to buy your widgets, you need to be sure you anticipate the questions that will need answers. Spell out what you have to offer, where and when it can be made available and what the cost will be. Prices are very important on the Web. Do not be reticent about giving prices, unless yours compare badly with those from other suppliers. A competitive price, clearly indicated and quoted in the appropriate currencies, can stop the window shopper in his or her tracks and clinch the business for you. In many cases, buyers will welcome the opportunity to place an order straight away, using an online order form.

But even if you have a policy of dealing with account customers only, or you do not have credit card transaction facilities, you should not allow the potential buyer to feel thwarted. If online trading is not possible, then make it very clear that you are keen to do business and what the next step is. Visitors to your site who leave feeling they have found new sources of supply and acquired information that will be useful to them will usually be back before long.

You've only got a minute or two, so use the time well

The basic facts of life on the Internet dictate that your site must make an impact in a very short time. Visitors to your home page must find something that interests them or promises a business benefit within the first minute and they need to be securely hooked inside two minutes or they will click on with their lives. The more familiar they are with the Net, the more abrupt and decisive they are likely to be in diving for the mouse button and moving on after a few seconds. People get into the habit of moving fast in this channel-hopper's paradise. And there is some justification for it. The sums involved may not be large, but it does cost money to look at your site. Many people are disproportionately aware of their online costs and train themselves to charge around the Net, hovering for as few seconds as possible at each destination. We have come across quite senior managers who flit about like this, fretting about the costs of ten minutes' research time on the Internet when they blithely spend far more on taxi fares every time they go out for a meeting.

Your site must look at least as good as your brochure

Think of the effort and investment of thought and money that goes into preparing your brochures. Then think of the amount of control you can exert over who gets hold of these brochures and what the context is. Compare this with the way anyone, anywhere on the planet, can connect up to your Website and view the imagery and information you have chosen to place there.

The idea that a site can be put together with less attention to strategic purpose, sales potential, brand building, copy quality and graphic impact than your brochure is ridiculous. Or it would be, if there weren't so many thousands of blatant examples of outrageously thoughtless, cheapskate, amateurish, sloppy and counterproductive work already in place on the Web. Second-rate graphics, limp copy and mistakes in the site design and building can be attributed to bad choices in the sourcing of professional skills. A site that doesn't know why it's there or what it's doing can only be blamed on poor management. And the Internet has a knack of ruthlessly exposing such weaknesses. There's always a lot of window shopping on the Web, because of the ease with which similar products from competing suppliers can be hunted down and compared side by side. In the physical world, your potential customer may not have access to your rival's brochure while looking at yours. In the cybermarket, you must assume that your sites will be slugging it out toe to toe.

Your home page must pack a punch

Whether it is conveyed in words or visuals, there must be something immediate and arresting about your home page. From the moment the screen fills, it needs to be working to your advantage, establishing a tone, starting to reinforce your brand values and giving the visitor some image or information that will surprise, please or at least engage the attention. Depending on your field of business, this may mean going for a wacky, youthful approach, with bright colours, eccentric typography and technical trickery such as animated sequences, or it could mean adopting a cool, restrained tone that implies a depth of quality and technical efficiency.

The occasional glaring mismatch between a company's true personality and its attempted embodiment on the Web can produce uncomfortably hilarious results. Corporate mutton dressed as entrepreneurial lamb is unlikely to fool anyone for long. The point is that the site must have a sense of conviction and integrity, while putting its message across emphatically and fast. If the home page has done its job, capturing the visitor's interest and offering a well-thought-out choice of routes to other relevant content on the site, you are at least in with a good chance of securing sales directly or, as the marketing experts so carefully phrase it, 'creating the preconditions for future sales'.

➡ SIX SLICK TIPS FOR BETTER BUSINESS

Finally, before we move on, in the next chapter, to the gentle art of choosing, briefing and steering Website designers, it's worth considering a handful of points that might be regarded as design matters, but are really much more to do with business efficiency and marketing effectiveness. On Web pages, more than in any other medium, design, content and purpose are – or should be – inextricably interwoven. Bearing these points in mind in your discussions with designers will help you ask the right questions and make sure that they don't get carried away in the sort of aesthetic arms race that leads to award-winning sites for them and an unproductive commercial liability for you.

1. Consider spreading your material over several pages, rather than piling it into one big one, so that your home page is quick to load.

2. Scatter navigation buttons wherever they might be useful,

pointing forwards, back and to your home page. It'll keep
your visitor's eyes where you want them, on your pages, and
they won't have to look up to the buttons on the browser.

3. Offer visitors a guestbook form, so they can choose to leave
   contact details. People like interactivity and if they are
   interested in your site, they may appreciate being alerted
   when you change the information on it. There's a paste-in
   guestbook template your people can lift, free, from
   GuestWorld (*http://www.guestworld.com*),
   which is already used on more than a million sites.

4. Encourage feedback by including an e-mail link on every
   page, so people don't have to go looking for it.

5. Always insist on printing out your home page and checking
   that it still looks passable in boring black and white, which
   is how most of those who want to keep your details will
   choose to print it out.

6. Remember that people who are short of time or using old
   equipment may well have chosen the 'no graphics' option.
   Make sure important information and links on your pages
   are clear, even with the graphics turned off.

Chapter 10
How to get the website you want

'Is it a fact – or have I dreamt it – that, by means of electricity, the world of matter has become a great nerve, vibrating thousands of miles in a breathless point of time?'

(Nathaniel Hawthorne, 1851)

➡ DON'T SHOOT THE MESSENGER

Since the commercial use of the Internet started to gain real momentum, round about mid 1996, the number of new sites has rocketed and the number of firms touting for business as Website designers has doubled and redoubled every year or so. The result has been a Wild West free-for-all, with a lot of companies parting with a lot of money for the privilege of launching ill-conceived, badly designed and poorly constructed sites.

In a chaotic market, where no-one has more than four or five years' experience and many small design groups are clearly using their clients' budgets to learn on the job, there are already plenty of companies feeling burnt and disillusioned. They have tried the Web and believe they have proved it doesn't work for them. But this is nothing more than a classic high-tech instance of shooting the messenger. It is like saying that television, or print advertising, or off-the-page marketing, will never work for a particular product or company, after trying one tentative experimental campaign in a field where there are few experts and many snake-oil salesmen.

There is already a mountain of evidence that publicising products and services on the Web can lead to explosive business growth, dramatic reductions in sales costs and ecstatically positive customer responses. There is nothing wrong with the medium. By late 1998, there were 500,000 companies doing business over the Internet, with an estimated 500 more joining them every day. And the spectrum of goods successfully marketed on the Web – from mountaineering kit, cars, flowers and jewellery to Barbie dolls, garden tools, engineering gaskets, telephone exchange equipment and hot meals – makes it highly unlikely that any product sectors will eventually prove to be Web-free zones.

➡ WHO'S GOING TO BUILD YOU THE SITE YOU NEED?

If your company has not yet ventured into this new commercial universe and feels the time is now ripe to make a move, the big question is always going to be: 'Who will be given the job of creating your site?'

The answer that tempts many beginners towards unhappy and misleading experiences is to hand the project over to one or two people inside the company, 'so that it won't cost much and we can keep an eye on what's going on'. It is true that there are now some very clever tools that can help the careful amateur put together a tidy and robust Website, but we would not recommend this approach. You can buy a professional specification video camera in any High Street, but how often do you see amateur camcorder footage that looks remotely professional? The gloss and finish that characterise good video work and good Website design come from the way the technical resources are used, rather than just having access to the latest tools and equipment. Unless you happen to have a rare combination of marketing, design and technical skills available to you, we can guarantee that your in-house effort will end up with a distinctly hand-knitted look, which will do your brand imagery no good at all.

Having dismissed the idea of growing your own, however, you are immediately faced with the problems of finding someone on the outside with the right skills, brainpower and integrity to produce a site for you that is worth showing to the world. Professional Web design groups will normally want to talk in terms of an absolute minimum of £1500 to £2000, for a small, simple site of three or four pages, and may come back to you with ambitious quotes of up to £100,000 or even more, accompanied by a barrage of good reasons why just dipping your toe in the water may do you more harm than good. Bear in mind that the bigger design groups will always be looking for high-value projects, to cover their higher overheads and leave themselves room for a generous profit, while the smallest designers may be cheap because they are inexperienced or incompetent. As is the case when you have to choose other suppliers of professional skills, such as PR agencies, systems integrators or brochure design groups, you are buying an end-product that does not yet exist – and there is plenty of scope for disappointment, if you make the wrong choice.

http://www.euromarc.com
The Euromarc Communications site brings together a lot of sound advice about marketing, strategy and Web design, with useful research data as well

➡ HOW DO YOU CHOOSE THE RIGHT DESIGNER?

There is a theory, of course, that you get what you pay for. It would be nice if that were true. The fact is, in a market that has attracted its fair share of get-rich-quick operators, high prices are no guarantee of quality. Good people will be aware of their worth and charge accordingly; charlatans will try to match them, in order to confuse the issue and make a good living. Everyone who comes to see you will promise the earth, explain how he or she has the team that can make your site really stand out, show you impressive examples of past work and offer references. And, after meeting three or four such designers, you will probably not be a great deal clearer about who you would feel confident with.

In the end, other things being equal, you will have to back your own judgement about the personalities involved and plump for the designer you believe is most likely to treat you and your project with real commitment, integrity and sensitivity to your needs. But there are plenty of preparations you can make beforehand that will help to narrow the odds.

➡ THE BRIEF IS FOR YOUR BENEFIT

First of all, before even inviting any designers to come and meet you, it is important to clarify your own thinking. The best way to do this is to spend some time developing a clear and detailed briefing document for the design work. This should specify what you want your Website to achieve, what business benefits you expect to derive from it, who your target audience is and how you see the site fitting in with the rest of your company's marketing communications mix.

The brief should come up with definite answers to all the big strategic questions, such as:

- Is your site intended to present your company to the world – or your products?
- Is it meant to create long-term demand for your goods and services or capture immediate online sales?

- Does it need to tie in with existing advertising themes or future campaigns?

- Is it aimed at existing customers, new prospects, suppliers and business partners or the general public?

- Must it speak to an international audience in other languages, as well as English?

But your brief should also consider the broad technical parameters, and the budget constraints that may influence them:

- How big will your Website be? Does it need to carry the equivalent of 10 A4 pages of information or 50?

- Will it be made up of text and graphics, or will it include animation and sound, live video feeds, full multimedia or fancy stuff like virtual reality modelling?

- Will you want to include a network of hypertext links to and from sites owned by your business partners?

- Will your pages contain live information that needs to be automatically updated in real time?

- Does your site need to offer credit card payment facilities?

➡ PUT THE CANDIDATES IN THE FIRING LINE

Once you know the answers to these key questions, you can begin your search for a design group that can make it all happen. You will naturally want to see three or four candidates, if only to get a realistic feel for what's on offer. But it may be useful to have a checklist to hand, to clarify exactly what you are looking for. So here are the essential questions to bear in mind when choosing Website designers:

1. Will my site look good and have a sharp, distinctive and appropriate design, reinforcing our established brand values?
2. Am I being shown evidence of the technical skill needed to make sure the programming features that really engage the

audience work properly – things such as animation, questionnaires and the customised Java programs that can be used to create links to stock databases or other information we may want to share with customers?

3. Am I confident that these people can help us think through how the site can complement our overall marketing strategy?

4. Do the designers have practical ideas about taking advantage of the unique features of the Web as a medium, such as its interactive potential?

5. Are the designers taking part in the pitch going to be the ones working on my project once the contract is awarded?

Another practical matter that's worth asking about – and one which will also give you some idea of how realistic and business-oriented the designers really are – is the issue of how anyone is supposed to know your new Website is there. A site that no-one sees is obviously a complete waste of money, but a site that the wrong people see is hardly any better. A competent and experienced team will approach this problem from at least two angles, looking at how the new site is flagged up in the physical world (in your advertising, in brochures and on your packaging) and in the virtual context, on the Internet. Some Web design firms will offer a standard service, guaranteeing to promote your site on 30 or 40 selected directories and search engines, or a more expensive effort that undertakes to promote it on all the relevant directories and search engines.

Do not be too impressed by all this. Submit It (*http://www.submit-it.com*), the largest service of its type, with over 250,000 customers, offers site owners the opportunity to announce their new Websites to their choice of more than 400 search engines, directories and 'what's new?' sites, sorted under 30 different category headings, for a modest payment of $60 (£37). It will even enable you to announce your Website to twenty well-known search engines and 'What's new?' sites (including AltaVista, InfoSeek, NetFind and WebCrawler) completely free of charge, in the hope that it will eventually be able to sell you some of its other marketing and analysis services for site owners.

➡ **WHOSE SIDE IS THE REFEREE ON?**

Everyone who is seriously interested in winning your business will name-drop like mad about previous clients and suggest that you should contact one or two of them as references. This is a cat and mouse game and you should be aware of what is going on. The design group that has worked for a major corporation and does not nominate this company as a reference site may have something to hide. You could always ask, directly, why such a prestigious client has not been suggested as a reference. The designer will try to steer you towards the company where his or her team has achieved the most emphatic success, and towards the individual in that company with whom the most friendly relationship was established. But the person who commissioned the site and worked most closely with the designers is not necessarily the one you should talk to.

For a more dispassionate view of how the Website has performed in relation to its business objectives, you may want to contact the marketing director, or even the chief executive, of the client company. Whoever you get in touch with, ask whether deadlines and budgets were respected. You should also try to find out how the design group performed after the big cheque had been handed over and cashed. Did the designers work hard to maintain the site and keep it interesting and up to date? If they did, it tells you a lot about their professionalism. If they didn't, it doesn't mean that they are not capable of setting up a good site for you. But it does mean you are likely to be on your own once the invoice is paid and the builders have moved on in search of bigger and better projects.

Chapter 11
The future is calling

'Chaos often breeds life, where order breeds habit.'

(Henry Adams, 1907)

➡ WHY ARE WE WAITING?

The Internet we will have tomorrow will spit and sizzle like rain on a hot shovel. But the Internet we have today often appears to be excruciatingly slow. University students and employees of large corporations that operate powerful in-house networks and have permanently open high-speed connections to the Net will disagree. They are used to a level of access that home users and people in most small businesses have never experienced. Yet their idea of what the present-day Internet is like is actually more accurate than the jaundiced views of the less privileged. And some of the new technologies that are waiting in the wings promise levels of speed and capacity that are hard to imagine today.

Three of these new approaches – enhanced cable TV networks, digital subscriber lines and Sprint's ION (integrated on-demand network) – offer download speeds at least 30 times faster than we are used to with traditional dial-up modem connections. If their developers' plans for fast roll-out during 1999 and 2000 always looked a little ambitious, we can be fairly sure that they will be widely available options, in Britain as well as in the USA, by 2005. We will be looking at these, and other hopes for a high-speed future, later in this chapter.

For the moment, though, we have to live with the technology that's here, around us. For all its faults – and no-one's denying that bottlenecks and overloaded servers do slow things up from time to time – the Net itself usually runs pretty fast. There are occasional traffic jams on the long-distance backbone connections, queues of packets waiting to be switched at various routers and even breakdowns at International Exchange Points like MAE East, the biggest in America (and therefore the world), which has caused major disruption whenever it has had to be closed for mainte-nance. These all have knock-on effects, and because there's no-one in charge of the Net, there's no-one to blame and nobody to complain to, which makes it all doubly frustrating. Hold-ups or slow-downs at this level are effectively on a par with Acts of God, as far as ordinary businesses are concerned. There is simply nothing anyone can do. But a lot of the problems that are blamed on the Internet have their origins much closer to home. Those of us who are making do with dial-up connections over ordinary telephone lines and who are sometimes left waiting for minutes on end for a Web page to download may well be contributing to our own discomfort.

➡ WHO PUT THE BRAKES ON?

Your choice of Internet access provider may be one factor, since the service any provider can offer depends largely on how many customers it has per modem. The higher the ratio of modems to customers, the better the service you will get. Then you – and all the other satisfied customers – will mention this excellence to friends and colleagues and people in your area will rush to join your service provider, thus lowering the ratio again and automati-cally making the service worse, until the next equipment upgrade, when the cycle will start all over again.

Then there's the first link in the telecommunications chain. That copper wire connection from your building out into the street and off to the exchange is a narrow pipe at the best of times. It is prone to noise and interference, which will slow down your connection speed, and those same wires may well have been in place for 40 years, so they will rarely be capable of delivering anything like their theoretical capacity. The further you are from your local exchange, the worse the signal will be.

Getting even closer to home, if you have an old and feeble PC, without much RAM (a 66 Mhz 486 with 8 Mb RAM is a very basic minimum for browsing today's complex Websites) and little space to spare on your hard disk, that will slow you right down, as will using an old operating system. A modem with a top speed of anything less than 28.8 Kbps is a recipe for frustration, too, even though your modem is never likely to enjoy the ideal conditions that would enable it to achieve its rated speed. Even the newest 56 Kbps modems only ever manage about 45 Kbps, on a good day.

Where several of these factors are combining to undermine overall performance, it's no wonder the whole process can feel dauntingly slow, even for the private individual who is just surfing for fun. For those who use the Internet for business, even in very small firms or working from home, the waste of time and energy and the increased phone bills that come with slow-motion browsing provide a strong argument for doing something about it.

➡ WHAT CAN I DO?

If staring at the screen while you wait for Web pages to load is driving you round the bend, there are two ways you can tackle the problem. The first approach is to change what you do, which isn't going to work miracles, but does have the advantage of being free and bringing immediate results. Here are four practical steps you can take to minimise the delays and frustrations:

- Download text only. When looking for straightforward information, click on 'options' and turn off the graphics and pictures that make many Web pages so slow to load. Switch off 'Auto load images' or 'Show pictures'.

- Get on the Net early in the morning (before 8 a.m. avoids BT's peak rate), when few Europeans are using it and the Americans are asleep. As the USA wakes up, the Internet slows down.

- Try pressing the 'Stop' and 'Reload/refresh' buttons to unlock pages that seem to have stopped loading.

- Many big commercial firms have 'mirror' sites in different parts of the world. If there's a mirror site near you, it will load much faster. Pick up a useful list of mirrors at TUCOWS (*http://www.tucows.com*).

The other approach is to begin to tackle the hardware aspects of the problem, which may involve spending a certain amount of money. There is a clear sequence of escalating investments you can make to improve matters, listed here with the cheapest measures first:

- Do a brisk bit of housekeeping to delete old and unwanted files (including killing all .tmp files), tidy up loose ends and free up more space on your hard disk. There are surprisingly easy instructions with Windows. (Cost: nothing.)
- Treat your PC to some more RAM, say another 16 Mb. (Cost: about £15.)
- Buy a new modem, preferably meeting the new V.90 56 Kbps standard. (Cost: about £90.)
- Upgrade to a new PC with a fast processor, 64 Mb of RAM, Windows 98, a larger, better screen and all sorts of new bells and whistles, including, quite probably, a 56 Kbps internal modem. (Cost: anything from £600 upwards.)
- Switch to an ISDN (digital) line for a much faster, cleaner connection. (Cost, including buying the terminal adapter that's needed instead of a modem: about £800 for the first year, plus call charges.)

➡ A WEB WITH NO LIMITS

For many people in business who have been eagerly awaiting the coming of better, faster ways of gaining access to the Internet, 1999 marks the turning point – the end of an era of relatively clunky, primitive connections for all but the most privileged corporate users and the beginning of an age of plenty. There are now at least three new or vastly improved technologies that were not widely available before 1999 that create the potential for wide, fast, affordable telecommunications pipes for smaller businesses and even for individuals: beefed-up cable TV networks, digital subscriber lines and the new ION (integrated on-demand network). All offer huge capacity and should, in due course, be within the budgets of ordinary firms and people at home.

http://www.norweb.co.uk
The future? If it works. Fast Net access for all via mains power lines is the goal of a pioneering system being tested by NorWeb and Northern Telecom

The catch is that the availability of high capacity access for millions of Internet users is a powerful incitement to inventive people to come up with new techniques and products that can produce spectacular multimedia effects by capitalising on the newly available bandwidth.

New capacity equals new traffic. It is the same problem that faces governments trying to plan workable motorway networks. Widen the M25 motorway around London to 14 lanes, as was proposed by Britain's tarmac-crazed Conservative government in the early 1990s, and you generate completely new traffic movements, as well as encouraging existing traffic to switch from other roads to your expanded M25. The result is a clogged, slow-moving motorway, much like the clogged, slow-moving motorway you set out to cure, only wider.

Add more bandwidth to people's Internet connections and you are sure to generate greater volumes of traffic per user, from more users, and a trend towards more bandwidth-hungry applications. As soon as most people are getting enough bits down the pipe to support full streaming (real-time) video, Website designers looking for maximum impact will naturally want to build action-packed, full-screen, colour video into their creations, whenever they can find the slightest justification for it.

In the long run, a technological version of Parkinson's Law will operate and traffic will expand to fill the space available. The problem of bandwidth constraints will not go away for ever. For the next few years, though, we can expect to enjoy something of a Golden Age, in which the capacity ordinary firms and individuals can access and afford is more than enough for all their immediate needs.

➡ FIVE HUNDRED TIMES FASTER WITH CABLE

It was the dramatic $48 billion (£29 billion) takeover of TCI, America's second-largest cable TV operator, by AT&T, the world's biggest long-distance telephone company, in June 1998, that signalled that cable was back in the limelight again. There are plenty of complications for the two US companies to overcome, not least because the cost of upgrading TCI's infrastructure to provide phone services and high-speed Internet access is estimated to be more than $15 billion, but AT&T clearly knew what it wanted. It had its corporate eye on the potential of TCI's big fat pipe, running into more than 20 million American homes and past another 30 million, as the conduit for phone calls, Internet access, TV, videophone links and all the other entertainment, information and business services AT&T expects to provide in the next few years.

Of all the technologies lining up as candidates for high-speed Internet access connections, only satellite links beat cable's potential capacity. The necklaces of low-orbit satellites starting operations in 2003 will offer incredible download speeds of up to 100 Mbps, anywhere on the earth's surface, but their services are unlikely to be cheap. Cable offers a less capital-intensive, less high-tech approach, but can still fizz data through at up to 30 Mbps, which must sound like heaven to anyone sitting waiting for a traditional dial-up modem to chug along 500 times slower than that.

Internet users in some parts of the USA can already take advantage of very fast cable modem access. It's not quite the theoretically possible lightning speed mentioned above. But it is, in practice, up to 30 times quicker at downloading a Web page than the best dial-up modem. 'It totally changes the experience,' said one of these cable modem pioneers. 'It makes surfing great again.'

There is a lot less cable installed in the UK than America and only 22 per cent of the homes that have potential access to cable TV have become subscribers, so cable connections to the Internet are not such an obvious option, especially outside the big cities. But Europe is a clear step ahead of America in digital cellphones and the new UMTS (universal mobile telephone service) standard will allow data connections via cellphones at speeds on a par with cable. UMTS licences granted in 1999 should mean that these services are operating in 2002, providing yet another route with the capacity to handle very demanding Internet services.

➡ POSITIVE IONS

It may be some years before high-speed satellite and cellphone links and the ultimate high bandwidth cable connections to the Internet are widely available. But while today's ISPs and online services can only offer their customers 56 Kbps or 33.6 Kbps connections, a different world is waiting just around the corner. In June 1998, the US telecoms company Sprint announced that it was launching a national network, scheduled to cover most of America's major cities by the end of 1999, that would offer 'almost unlimited' capacity over ordinary copper telephone wires to homes and small businesses. The new technology, known as ION (integrated on-demand network), should allow people to use the

Internet at up to 100 times the speed of today's modems, with Web pages flashing up almost as soon as you hit the button.

With that sort of speed available to everyone, ways of using the Web which are painfully cumbersome now could suddenly become quite acceptable. Instead of offering a poor imitation of the printed page, catalogues would be able to tempt shoppers with full screen, full colour, full motion sound and vision clips of the goods on sale, from clothes to cars to houses. Interactivity could be taken to completely new levels and trawling the Net for ill-defined snippets of information could become a pleasure, with responses snapping back just as fast as you could frame your questions. If the new system lives up to the fanfare with which Sprint and its business partners, including smart technology companies like Cisco and Bellcore, have launched it on the world, other telecoms companies are going to have to respond with comparable services before too long.

The speeds Sprint has boasted for ION (6 Mbps downstream, when you're downloading Web pages, and 1.5 Mbps upstream, for messages you send back) are considerably higher than anyone else is claiming over existing copper phone lines. But some of the regional 'Baby Bell' telephone companies in America have already started offering digital subscriber line services (DSL), over existing wires, which can shift bits at a very quick 1.5–2 Mbps. The approaches they have adopted are incompatible with each other, but all depend on adding a new 'pump' at the exchange end and a new black box on the customer's premises, to push through huge amounts of digitised information and give vastly increased capacity to old wires that may have been in place for 30 or 40 years.

➡ WHERE CULTURE AND TECHNOLOGY INTERACT, THE WALLS COME DOWN

Once technologies such as ION, enhanced cable and DSL have proved themselves in the American market, it is hardly likely that either businesses or enthusiastic individual Internet users in Britain and Europe would be content to plod along indefinitely at today's sedate pace.

In most matters to do with the Internet, Europe has tended to lag America by two to three years, but this gap is likely to close as the Web itself begins to speed up the transmission of ideas across national borders. One of the factors that has traditionally slowed down the spread of new ideas is the fact that most of the traditional mainstream media, including newspapers, magazines and television, have always been distinctly national in character. Language, culture, political and legal boundaries, physical geography and advertisers' market segmentation policies have all conspired with the inevitable jingoism to keep the barriers up. The few examples that have crossed these barriers – *Reader's Digest*, the old Radio Luxemburg, BBC World Service, CNN and MTV, *Vogue*, *The Economist* and *National Geographic* magazine – stand out as exceptions that prove the rule.

This time it is different. On the Internet, the user's perception of distance is precisely determined by the response times that are experienced. A Website in Chicago that appears on the screen quickly for a user in London or Los Angeles doesn't seem far away. A local weather or travel site that takes an age to materialise – whether it is the site owner's fault, or caused by a problem on the high-speed Internet backbone, or gremlins affecting the telephone line right outside the building – always feels as if it has been dragged in from the back of beyond. What's near is what you can get to. What's far is everything else.

The immediacy with which the Chicago pages pop up on your screen naturally encourages you to return to the site and feel some affinity with it. Once you have been there two or three times, it starts to feel familiar, a part of your world, rather than a disembodied set of electronic images sitting on a server thousands of miles away. The familiarity and accessibility of other people's thoughts, ideas, jokes, advertisements and opinions, coming to you on a medium that has no cultural bias at all towards the country you are in, is a factor that is bound to encourage the dissemination of ideas and expectations on a worldwide basis. If a technological breakthrough like ION means that millions of Americans find they can use the Web as a genuinely instantaneous resource, without all the tedious waiting around between pages, the rest of the Internet community will quickly begin to clamour for something similar.

➡ TAKE A WALK ON THE WIRED SIDE

What no-one knows is how much longer the apparatus on the end of your Internet connection is likely to be the PC that seems so universal today. Microsoft's WebTV service is already beginning to deliver the Internet on television to homes around the world, blurring the boundary between the PC and the TV and bringing the Internet out of the study or back bedroom and into the mainstream of family life. On a fully Web-enabled TV, the viewer will be able to watch EastEnders, click on the corresponding Website in a window on the screen for more information, while the programme is still going on, and even place an order to buy the jacket one of the characters is wearing or the CD that's playing behind the bar in the Queen Vic. There are already Web-enabled cellphones and personal organisers, cashpoint machines and airport information kiosks.

But as both the price and size of the basic building blocks of computing and telecommunications continue to shrink away to almost nothing, more startling products are on their way. Web-enabled toys in the pipeline include an Internet-linked Barbie doll, which will eventually take its place in the Mattel range alongside the interactive Winnie the Pooh that can download 20 minutes of personalised programmed speech from a PC, via a microwave link. Mattel is deadly serious about stuffing its established toys – including Cabbage Patch Dolls and Hot Wheels racers – with advanced technologies. It already has an agreement with Intel to develop interactive toys together, leading the director of consumer software for Intel's developer relations group, Michael Bruck, to wax lyrical about the potential of toys that can connect to the Net to get more information or to download more games. 'Technology is appealing to kids,' Bruck told journalists at the 1998 American International Toy Fair in New York. 'Half the people who buy computers for the home are families with kids – and they buy them for the children.'

It all underlines the point that we will soon be seeing objects, and not just people, wired up and communicating over the Web. Vehicles and parcels will be able to track their own movements. In industry, sensors of all kinds will be able to register and report temperature, pressure, vibration, light or dark – and the presence or absence of human beings in an office or room.

As standardisation and massive production runs make the cost of the devices fall to the point where they add only a few pence to the cost of any item, your coat or your briefcase will be able to check in and tell you where you left them. Your refrigerator will be able to monitor what is put into it and what is taken out, flagging up low stocks of regularly purchased items. Even your dustbin will be on the Web, the prophets say, so that it can recognise empty packaging you throw away and trigger the automatic ordering of replacement supplies. And if all this sounds a bit too George Orwell to take, we should remember that, apart from its most public manifestations, it is all likely to be under our personal control. We have choices. But if we don't exercise them at the right times, we could find ourselves living, all too soon, in an all-too-wired world.

➡ THE NET ISN'T GOING TO CRASH

This kind of development would obviously have implications for the capacity of the Internet. The amazing headless, shapeless, organic and unstoppable Net we know – 'the global brain', as Joe Firmage, whizkid chairman of the US Web consulting group (*http://www.usweb.com*) calls it – creaks at times, but is generally fairly effective at handling the needs of 100 million or so users. Even the Starr Report didn't bring it down. Technology is finding new ways every day to pump more and more bits down a given pipe and there is already an enormous reserve of unused fibre optic cabling, installed around the world. We have seen enough to know that the beginner's question, 'What if it all goes wrong and stops working?', is not the one we need to worry about and plan our future round, any more than we make contingency plans to carry on business without the world's telephone system. There was the one big phone crash on the American East Coast, in 1991, when 40 million people were effectively unplugged for 19 hours. But though a lot of assumptions were shaken by that incident, it did not seem to have any lasting effect on the way business organised its activities. We know that blizzards and earthquakes, floods and hurricanes will occasionally strike in the physical world, but it doesn't stop us dead in our tracks. In the same way, with the global networks, all we can do is take reasonable precautions, up to a certain level of cost, and then get on with our lives. As the entrepreneurs in Hong Kong used to say: 'If it's six years to 1997, that's time to make four fortunes.'

Back in the 1980s, years before the Web came into being, one of the top researchers at BT's famous Martlesham Heath laboratory complex uttered a prophetic line. 'The phone network is the biggest man-made creation on the planet,' he said. 'It's becoming the central nervous system for the world. The only thing is, it's not attached to anything resembling a brain.' The speaker, Peter Cochrane, went on to become Head of Research for BT, a *Daily Telegraph* and *Financial Times* columnist, a TV pundit and futurologist and author of an excellent and provocative book called *Tips for Time Travellers* (Orion Business, 1997). He also took the unusual step of placing masses of fascinating follow-up material on the Internet and invited readers and others to explore it on his personal Website (*http://www.labs.bt.com/people/cochrap/*).

Some years after the original 'central nervous system' remark, Cochrane came out with another key observation, to the effect that 'the way to make a network more valuable is to link it to another network'. Putting the two ideas together, it is obvious, in retrospect, that it is the Internet's bringing together of knowledge, intelligence and connectivity that has added value and made it such a bottomless reservoir of resources for our future.

Given that the Net can cope with the traffic generated by 100 million and more human users and their sporadic actions and requests for information, how will it handle the consequences of the wiring-up of my dustbin and your Christmas parcels? A universe in which there are millions of objects nattering away on the Web, alongside the people, could throw a completely different level of strain on the physical capacity of the Internet, creating new problems that would have to be taken very seriously.

➡ TOO SUCCESSFUL FOR ITS OWN GOOD?

The founding fathers of the Internet were a strange bunch, scattered in space and time, drawn from many different fields and often quite oblivious of each other's efforts. They were defence industry communications experts, particle physicists, Norwegian radar technicians and a host of university researchers. They were driven by an equally mixed collection of motives – patriotism, global utopianism, the idealistic thirst for knowledge, the ruthless pursuit of academic recognition and, often, overwhelming curiosity about what the emerging technologies of the computer age could achieve if they were put together in new combinations. What was conspicuously absent from the range of motives was the idea of profit. Indeed, until the ban on business use of the Net was lifted in 1991, even thinking about exploiting the Internet for profit was seen as a dastardly betrayal of this loose community's principles.

Now that commercial use of the Internet is beginning to catch fire, the visionaries are out ahead, as usual, looking for the answers to the future's big questions. If the build-up of chattering dustbins and Web-wise Barbie dolls and millions of other devices, all routinely communicating over the Net, takes us to the limits of its global capacity, what happens next? Will the Internet melt down and self-destruct? Can we expect the classic post-atomic-holocaust back-to-bows-and-arrows scenario? Will we be forced to give up on this modern Wonder of the World and return to basic phones and a two-day postal service?

➡ STAND BACK, HERE COMES INTERNET2

The positive answer to such questions may well turn out to be Internet2. This is a major collaborative project involving 120 US universities, run by a body called the University Corporation for Advanced Internet Development (UCAID) and backed by US federal grants and support from industry. The stated aim is to recreate the kind of conditions that led to the birth of today's Internet, with the universities collaborating to launch new ideas and carry them through the pre-commercial development phase.

'This is the approach that characterised the first Internet and it can work again today,' says one UCAID spokesman. 'A key goal of this effort is to accelerate the technology transfer necessary to move the appropriate technologies into the commercial sector, creating the basis of a next-generation network that will continue US leadership in this important area.' The world has been warned; there is an element of long-term economic imperialism underlying this investment. But then, anyone who thought the Americans would willingly give up their lead in this area clearly hasn't been paying attention, anyway. The line is that this technology that is good for America will also be good for the world, which is probably true.

After all, the chief characteristic of the World Wide Web is its openness. Because the Web is open to all sorts of computers, accessible by all sorts of people in all sorts of countries and usable for all sorts of purposes, the lead the Americans gained by being first to adopt the technology is not what really counts. What has put the US firmly in the leading role is the uninhibited energy, imagination and ingenuity with which its people and companies have set about exploiting the Net for fun and for profit. It's not having the technology – it's using it. Every refinement that becomes available in this area is disseminated very quickly. So if America's government, corporations and universities are combining to line up the sequel to the Internet success story, the rest of the world can only wish them luck with I2. We'll be getting the benefits soon enough.

Chapter 12
Right, let's make it happen

'Thinkers prepare the revolution. Bandits carry it out.'

(Mariano Azuela, 1918)

➡ BOOKMARKS TO CONJURE WITH

When you find a page on the Web that you're going to want to come back to, you can create a short cut, almost instantly, that will take you straight there. Just click on 'Bookmarks' or 'Favourites' (all right, we know it'll be spelt 'Favorites', but you can't compromise on everything) at the top of your browser window and click 'Add' in the drop-down menu. You can be quite indiscriminate about this – you're not making a long-term commitment and you can delete bookmarks almost as easily as you create them.

Here are a couple of lists of useful, thought-provoking or simply enjoyable Websites you should visit, some of which you will almost certainly want to bookmark for future reference. The first list consists of resources and examples that may be useful to you in a business context. The second is more of a Magical Mystery Tour, made up of sites that we've found or people have pointed us towards that either make life easier or make you feel good.

➡ THE WEB MEANS BUSINESS: A TOP TEN WITH WORK IN MIND

1. *http://www.fastcompany.com* – Inspiring stuff for both you and your business from cool US magazine.

2. *http://www.unitedmedia.com/comics/dilbert* – Simple reportage in

words and pictures, though people will keep trying to read things into it.

3. *http://www.botham.co.uk* – Famous pioneering UK small business site, set up by in-house enthusiast at upper crust craft bakery in Whitby.

4. *http://www.zdu.com* – Online Web techniques university from techno publishers Ziff Davis, complete with Campus Store, Student Union and Library. Carvery-style menu of Web skills training – $7.95 a month, for as many courses as you want.

5. *http://magna.com.au/~prfbrown/albert_e.html* – Grab some wisdom with Einstein's greatest quotes.

6. *http://babelfish.altavista.com* – Amazing new language robot site, giving free and instant translations between English and five other languages. Makes amusing howlers, but still very handy if your Portuguese isn't quite up to scratch.

7. *http://www.anonymizer.com* – A brisk lesson in Internet security. 'We already know about you', the site says. And, sure enough, they do. Unless you're coming from behind a company firewall, you'll see details pop up like what browser and operating system you are using, who your service provider is and even which site you last visited.

8. *http://www.volvocars.volvo.co.uk* – Searchability is a major theme on the Web. Track down a really sensible second-hand car with a quick scan across stocks in every Volvo dealer.

9. *http://www.botspot.com* – Robot warren where you can get yourself an intelligent agent that will scurry round the Web on your behalf and do your research for you.

10. *http://www.odci.gov/cia/publications/pubs.html* – The CIA's World Factbook. Detailed up-to-date info on every country under the sun. Get your facts from the people who make it their business to know.

➡ THE MAGICAL MYSTERY TOUR: A BAKER'S DOZEN FOR YOU

1. *http://www.shopsonthenet.co.uk*, *http://www.shoppingservice.de*, *http://www.le-shop.ch* – UK shops, German shops, Swiss shops.

Compare, contrast and check out the prices.

2. *http://www.salonmagazine.com* – The best and coolest online culture e-zine. Unlike many, it talks the talk without disappearing up its own pretensions.

3. *http://www.gorp.com* – Stands for Great Outdoor Recreational Page. Turn off that machine and get some fresh air.

4. *http://www.electra.com* – Bright, career-minded women's site from AOL. New, but hit its stride quickly with a plausible magazine format.

5. *http://www.db-ag.de/home_e/f-engl.htm* – Create fantasy railway journeys all across Europe. Try Aberdeen to Lodz in Poland – six changes and 31 hours.

6. *http://www.designersdirect.com* – Calvin Klein online. And Tommy Hilfiger, Versace, Gucci, Oakley, Levi Strauss, Polo, DKNY, Joe Boxer and Dolce & Gabbana.

7. *http://www.mymenus.com* – Vast, varied and ingenious selection of recipes.

8. *http://www.football365.com* – Real, properly written and edited, daily football newspaper that you really can pre-customise to get what you want. A technical triumph.

9. *http://www.bargainholidays.com* – Just what you wanted. All the main operators (28 of them, with updates direct from their computers) and everything that's going in the next 12 weeks.

10. *http://www.anorak.co.uk* – Daily selection of daft stories culled from the UK papers. Bits and pieces from the redtops and the broadsheets and some that never made it into print.

11. *http://www-psych.nmsu.edu/~vic/faceprints/female_study.html* – Is this the most beautiful face in the world? See the composite face evolved in a huge international Internet-based experiment by New Mexico State University's FacePrints program. Surprisingly, you can glimpse what they mean in this hauntingly vacant image.

12. *http://www.timecast.com* – Live, on-the-fly audio and video is everywhere on the Web now, with rock concerts, radio and TV stations.

13. *http://www.learn2.com* – The site that calls itself 'the ability utility'. Learn to do anything, from mending the roof or a scratched CD to baking bread, shaving better, or soundproofing teenagers' rooms.

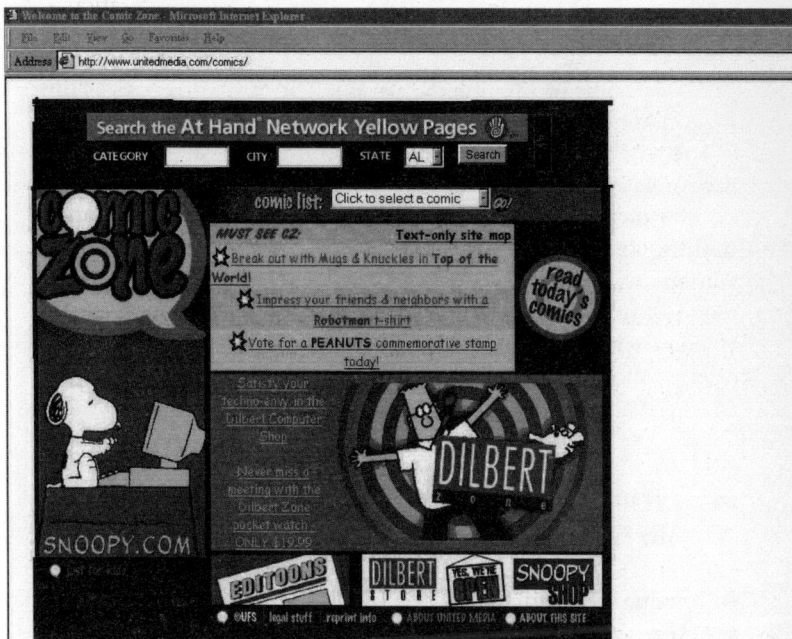

http://www.unitedmedia.com/comics
Not just the post-rightsizing management gospel according to Dilbert, but daily fun and philosophy from Peanuts and other popular strips

➡ WILL ALL THE PRIZES GO TO THE BIG BOYS?

No-one would really expect the birth of a new business medium to change the way the world is. The rich – the companies that can afford to pay for the best brains, the best technology, the best design teams and the most powerful and ubiquitous marketing campaigns – are always likely to get richer, as long as they don't completely lose the plot.

Yet one of the unexpected bonuses from the birth of the Internet has been the new lease of life that it has given to small firms that have had the initiative to grasp its potential. Of course, there are plenty of Internet-related start-ups – any significant new technology spawns opportunities for the young and the energetic to flex their entrepreneurial muscles and go all out for the fast buck. But it is the revitalisation of older, more established businesses that has emerged as a striking aspect of the Web's first few years and has produced some heartening tales of small firms striking back against juggernaut competitors.

The key to this is the simple fact that all sites are equally accessible on the Web. Big Business can spend as much as it likes on the design and construction of its sites, and fill them with flashing lights, twirling animations, high definition graphics and sumptuous sounds. But this is all in vain if the potential customer does not turn up to view it. And the people who use the Web tend to know what they are looking for and go where they choose, with a sometimes perverse resistance to the efforts of large corporations to lure them in.

➡ EVENING THE ODDS IN THE BATTLE AGAINST THE SUPERMARKETS

In Britain, for example, the butchers' trade has taken a pounding over the past few years – and not just because of the BSE and *E. coli* health scares. Across the country, local traditional, family-owned butcher's shops have been going out of business at an alarming rate, as supermarket chains such as Tesco (the well-known food store, bank and, now, Internet service provider), Sainsbury and Asda have focused more of their attention on fresh foods, brightly packaged and presented and sold at price levels local butchers can seldom match. But keen though the supermarket prices may be, these retail giants cannot provide what everybody wants.

There are dissident voices that claim supermarket bacon has no flavour and loses 50 per cent or more of its weight in the pan, that the chicken tastes like fish (and the fish tastes of nothing) and that the standardised cuts of pork and beef, in their clingfilm wrapping, look a lot more appetising than they taste. While most of us shrug and buy what we are offered, these diehards, representing just a few per cent of the people in each supermarket's area, are beginning to emerge as a market that can keep traditional butchers' shops alive. It's true that the specialist butcher must usually draw on a wider catchment area to piece together enough of a customer base to stay afloat, but people have become increasingly willing to drive a few more miles to get what they want.

Now, with the resources and search facilities of the Web to help them, they do not have to rely on word-of-mouth recommendation to find a butcher who can offer them pedigree beef, hand-made sausages, dry cured bacon or a range of organic meat. Running a quick search on Excite (*http://www.excite.com*), for example, leads to an interesting site called the Food Links Page (*http://www.users.globalnet.co.uk/~proven/pages/food2.htm*), which contains links to sites run by specialist traditional butchers in Hereford & Worcester, Yorkshire, Cumbria and Scotland and an organic butcher in Somerset that can even supply organic pet food.

For a 90-year-old business like Jack Scaife Ltd of Keighley, West Yorkshire, it was not an obvious step to start offering bacon and black pudding online. Yet only two years after launching his site, owner Chris Battle found that customers arriving via the Web (*http://www.classicengland.co.uk/scaife.html*) were buying one tonne of bacon from him every week. They came from the North of England, from London and the Home Counties, from Europe and from all over the world, including the occasional order from Africa and the Far East.

While this kind of expansion into national and world markets is not going to be possible or desirable for many of the small butchers threatened by the power of the big retail chains, it does illustrate the ability of the Internet to bring together the specialist vendor and the selective buyer, in defiance of questions of location and geography. What works across thousands of miles is increasingly likely to work in a local area, closer to home, if only because of the rapidly growing density of the Web-connected population and people's burgeoning awareness that they can get what they want – and often pay the prices they want to pay – by tapping into the resources of the Web.

In the next few years, we may well see the end of the pessimistic assumption that the butcher, baker or candlestick maker who finds a new supermarket opening up across the road is automatically finished. As long as either the goods or the service provided by the specialist offer customers something the supermarket can't match, survival is a real possibility.

➡ HOME PAGE OR YELLOW PAGES?

Part of the problem, in the past, has been the difficulty of keeping the small business's offering visible to potential customers, particularly in sectors where the goods or services are not purchased regularly. Most conventional advertising is expensive and gone all too soon from the newspaper pages and poster sites. But a modest Website is cheap to set up and maintain and has the sort of long-term presence that has always made Yellow Pages especially attractive to small, local businesses, with the important difference that it can convey vastly more information.

As looking for what you need on the Web becomes as familiar as using the Yellow Pages directory, almost any small firm that is clear about its USP (unique selling proposition) and bright enough to put it across attractively will discover that customers now have a better way to get in touch.

For the emergency plumber who wants to steal a march on his local rivals, becoming the first name that pops up on Yahoo!'s UK search engine (*http://www.yahoo!.co.uk*) when a worried householder searches for 'plumber Blackpool' or 'leak 24 hours Swindon' is going to be a real business advantage – and you can do it without having to rename your business AAAA Aardvark Plumbing Services to elbow your way to the top of the heap.

The geographical factor is vital. No-one wants to call in a plumber from 20 miles away, so there are entrepreneurial opportunities here for plumbers – and couriers, plasterers, landscape gardeners, photographers, undertakers, roof repairers, locksmiths, and people in any number of service trades – in every town and district in the country. What's more, until others cotton on to this new way of making the connection between the plumber and the plumbed, the firms that promote themselves on the Web early on will have the field to themselves, in what amounts, in advertising terms, to a solus position. The demographics of the Internet ensure that the customers that come to you via this new route will be, in the main, well-heeled and able to pay for your services. In the case of distress purchases, such as calling in plumbers to fix a leak or unblock a drain, they are also likely to be convinced of your professionalism by your presence on the Internet and by the reassuringly informative tone of your Website.

This is not just window-dressing, either. In a traditional directory, people looking for emergency plumbers often have to take a chance on someone about whom they know virtually nothing but a name and a telephone number.

Even a small, very basic Website can give customers an address, several contact numbers, lists of the sort of work you do, details of your charging and guarantee policies, public liability insurance and affiliations to professional bodies, names and photographs of key staff (a definite advantage if the situation involves opening the door in the middle of the night) and even, perhaps, a list of business or domestic customers locally who have given permission to be used as references. That is genuine added value for the anxious customer. It is also so unusual that it is bound to get your customers talking to their friends and neighbours about your firm and therefore win you the most valuable promotional asset of all, word-of-mouth publicity.

➡ LET YOUR PROSPECTS QUALIFY THEMSELVES

Compared with the shrill shouting match of the Yellow Pages and other business directories, this can be an elegantly effective way to attract new custom. And the economics of starting and running a Website make sound sense for all kinds of small businesses in the service trades.

It is true, of course, that you can only communicate via the Web with a small subset of the total population in your area. Though the proportion of the population with Internet access, either at home or at work, is rising fast, it will be years before you can hope to reach even half the people who live in your catchment zone. And you cannot get through to anyone, anywhere, if the computer is not switched on. On the other hand, this is not like broadcasting a TV commercial. You are not hurling your information at 5 million people, in the knowledge that 4,930,000 will totally ignore your advert and the hope that a fair number of the remaining 70,000 will be thinking about buying your product or service some time soon.

The big difference is that the only people who will find you will be people who are looking for you. They are a self-selecting audience. If you send out a reasonably attractive direct mail campaign, for example, to a list of 100 people, you expect to receive coupons back from perhaps two or three. Send to 20,000 and you'll usually get about 400 to 500 responses. That is your initial selection process. From that group of responders, you then have to try to weed out the cranks, the compulsive responders, the comparison shoppers who've also replied to all your competitors' mailshots and the indecisive people who thought they might want to buy but have now decided to spend the money on something else. What's left is a tiny group of real prospects. If you can sell to them, the exercise was worthwhile. If not, you go back and start again.

On the Web, the dynamics of making a sale can be very different. Sometimes people will have thrust a cluster of keywords at a search engine with little real hope of finding what they want and will be absolutely delighted to see one or two appropriate hot links appear in the results list. Sometimes they will have a vague idea that your firm exists, but not be able to remember what you are called, where you are based or anything that might usefully help them get in touch with you ('Oh yes, they do hand-made rocking horses and they're somewhere in the West Country, aren't they?'). Sometimes they will be looking for a supplier or tradesperson who meets one particular criterion ('I don't want anyone who isn't registered with the trade association') or who is near enough to offer responsive after-sales support.

In all these cases, the potential customer is actively seeking someone to do business with. Your conversion rates for prospective customers who contact you via the Website will never be 100 per cent, but they can be startlingly good. One reason is that other people will have quietly paid a visit, looked at what's on your site, decided it's not right for them and slipped away. This is something you can track, incidentally, with good cheap software like Web-Trends (£200 or so, from *http://www.webtrends.com*), or by paying a few pounds extra for a statistics package from your site's Web host. The people who do take it further and contact you, either by e-mail from your site or by picking up the phone, are the ones who are already close to giving you their business. And because they will probably know a great deal more about you and your product or services than people who have arrived via Yellow Pages, they are also likely to be more decisive and take up less of your time.

➡ PAINLESS PAGES FOR DENTAL PIONEERS

The key question in all this, for all very small businesses contemplating the idea of tiptoeing out onto the Web is 'How much is it going to cost?'

Perhaps the clearest indication that it needn't cost much is the fact that there are now about 40 dental practices in the UK (and more than 1200 in the US) with their own Websites. Dental surgeries are a fine example of stable, low-key local businesses, with roots (ouch!) in the community and, usually, few ambitions to take over the world. Until recently, they were not allowed to advertise their presence, so there are not many that would claim to be experts at marketing themselves. But with a little goading from two energetic online services – DERWeb, the Dental Educational Resources on the Web site run by the University of Sheffield (*http:// www.derweb.ac.uk*), and Dentanet (*http://www.dentanet.org.uk*), an online forum maintained and developed by the Dental Practice Board and IBM (UK) – the dental community is gradually being introduced to the idea of marketing on the Internet.

Both organisations offer help, hand-holding and professional Web design services to dentists, dental laboratories and others in their industry. But it is Dentanet that has cleverly designed fixed-price, minimum-cost packages to persuade cautious newcomers to take their first steps. It offers dentists a Practice Website package for a set-up fee of £100 and an annual charge of £25 (plus VAT), to include six pages, up to ten photos or graphics, apart from the practice logo, 750 words of text and a hypertext link from the online Find-a-Dentist service, so that people searching for a surgery in a particular area are brought straight to the practice's home page.

In case even that's too big a commitment for a tentative beginner, Dentanet also offers an alternative: a Practice Home

Page, with just 150 words, basic details of staff and opening times, two pictures and the hotlink, for a £50 set-up fee and £10 a year. Both the Practice Website and Practice Home Page deals take care of design and Website hosting and maintenance, give dentists their own Web addresses (in the form *http://www.dentanet.org.uk/ practicename*) and allow reasonable amendments to details to allow for staff turnover and other changes during the year.

At these prices, the experiment of launching out onto the Web involves far less expenditure than the large display advertisements many dental practices routinely take in the Yellow Pages directory, at a cost of several hundred pounds for a year's exposure in a crowded and competitive local market. While the dental Websites may be simple and unspectacular, compared with some of the extrovert, attention-grabbing designs to be seen elsewhere, the fact that half a dozen practices have the whole field to themselves in London, for example, must be good for business.

➡ A NEW ROLE FOR TRADE ASSOCIATIONS

If Dentanet can help dentists make the transition to Web-based marketing, there must be scope for many other professional and trade bodies to put together cheap and cheerful packages to help their members move towards the Internet. Solicitors could certainly benefit from such a scheme, possibly organised for them by the Law Society. You can see a good example of an enterprising family solicitor's Website from Fidler & Pepper in Nottingham (*http://www.fidler.co.uk*), but this is very much the exception – and it clearly isn't a £100 job, with its online quotes and progress reports for conveyancing and its interactive forms for accident victims considering compensation claims. Mark Slade of Fidler & Pepper says the site has paid for itself 'over and over and over' in its first three years, but estimates that commissioning a comparable Website now would cost several thousand pounds. 'You'd probably get quotes ranging from £3000 to £15,000,' he says. Only about 350 of the thousands of small legal firms in Britain have made an appearance on the Internet so far, along with 50 or so chambers or individual barristers, but it is almost certain that most solicitors' practices will want to have some presence on the Web in the next two or three years.

For small businesses and professional firms of all kinds, there are going to be real marketing opportunities on the World Wide Web. There will also be opportunities to get it wrong. Some firms will be ripped off by incompetent Web designers cashing in on their anxiety as they hurry to avoid missing the boat. Others will simply miss it and see business leak away as looking on the Internet becomes more familiar as a way of sourcing goods and services, at work and at home. Trade associations and professional bodies, buying groups and marketing co-operatives can all do their more hesitant members a favour by providing or arranging low-cost, low-risk routes onto the Web. If these bodies cannot take the task on, they can, at least, help enormously by identifying trusted and approved suppliers who are prepared to work within format and budget guidelines that can be settled in advance.

➡ WE HAVE LIFT-OFF

The Internet is a tool for businesses of every size. Anyone can afford to use it – and any company that decides not to use it needs to do so with its eyes wide open and an awareness of the possible consequences.

In the six months up to the end of 1998, it became clear that business on the Net had suddenly and abruptly achieved the long-awaited critical mass, with consumers signalling by their actions that they were no longer panicked about the possibility of credit card fraud if they tried to buy from online shops. From this point on, the snowball can only grow, bigger and bigger, faster and faster, as the growth of online business creates its own momentum and its own new set of opportunities. The tools and technologies the Web has spawned are underpinning astonishing, phenomenal growth in the use of intranets within companies and the increasingly intricate cross-linking networks of extranets and ultranets that tie businesses ever closer to their trading partners. And because these tools are both easy to use and powerful, they have been snatched from the experts and grasped by ordinary people with no technical knowledge, in a way that has never happened before since computers were invented. Revolutions occur when a mass of people, fired with new ideas, look down and see they have the weapons in their hands to make dreams come true. The Internet has armed us for a future that is wildly unpredictable, but full of limitless promise, for big organisations, small companies and the individuals with the verve to go to meet it head-on.

Appendix A
Do we need to worry about viruses and hackers?

'Hush, hush, hush, here comes the bogey man.'

(Henry Hall, 1936)

➡ WORRY YES, FRET NO

Computer viruses – alongside hackers, pornography, credit card fraud and addictive surfing – are part of the black mythology of the Internet. Fear of all of them is regularly stoked up by the tabloid press. But whereas Internet-crazed surfing addicts and verifiable cases of online credit card fraud are so hard to find that we can treat the dangers as non-existent and averagely aware adults should easily be able to avoid encountering any pornographic material, viruses and hackers definitely do exist. There are thousands of known and recognised computer viruses (one of the leading anti-virus products claims to protect against more than 18,000 of them) and thousands of nosey or malicious hackers. What matters, however, is how much of a threat they pose to you and your business.

Viruses are small, self-replicating pieces of computer code inserted into otherwise innocent programs. Contrary to popular belief, they don't all demolish your data files, clog up your memory and make your hard drive unusable. Some, in fact, are quite harmless bits of fun – they make your computer sneeze once a year or bring up a facetious message across the screen for a few seconds and then make it disappear again. Some may be a pain in the neck but are obviously born out of deeply held convictions. There's a virus called Nuclear, for example, that inserts 'Stop French nuclear testing in the Pacific' into everything you print. But many are downright destructive and show a vicious ingenuity that demands a determined response. Good, regularly updated antivirus software can be bought on disk or downloaded from the Web, though it goes without saying that this is one program you must only pick up from a totally reliable, trusted and recommended site. Norton AntiVirus Deluxe (£45) (*http://www.symantec.com/avcenter/index.html*), Dr Solomon's AntiVirus Toolkit (£81, including quarterly update CDs, details at *http://www.drsolomon.com*) and McAfee VirusScan Security Suite (about £42) (*http://www.mcafee.com*) are all popular and dependable tools, while Microsoft (*http://www.microsoft.com/office/antivirus* for advice and products) has more reasons than most to make sure PC virus activity doesn't get out of hand. The best virus-checkers run unobtrusively in the background and snap into action automatically to scan every file you run or copy. They are all modified every few weeks to take account of each new virus, with updates that can often be downloaded free by existing customers.

➡ JUST LOOKING IS SAFE ENOUGH

The first point to make clear is that you won't acquire an infection just by looking, either at a Website or at an ordinary piece of e-mail that arrives in your mailbox. But opening e-mail attachments is always potentially dangerous, unless you are quite sure about the source.

Most modern viruses (over 2000 different varieties, at the last count) are designed to lurk inside macros in Microsoft Word or Excel files and are activated as soon as you open the infected document or spreadsheet. Other common ways of catching viruses are by copying material from other people's floppies, running programs downloaded from online discussion groups and – sad, but true – transferring disks backwards and forwards between your machine and a poorly maintained corporate network. Files with the .exe extension and any spreadsheets or word processed documents that might contain contaminated macro programs must always be scanned with a virus-checker, but pictures, plain text files and video should all be perfectly safe.

Despite all the noise and hype, the chances of being hit by a virus are low anyway, and very low indeed if you use an up-to-date virus-checker. And the chances of being bothered by a random hacker are minute. Unless your business is conspicuous, controversial and apt to draw attention to itself in ways that arouse the ire of the Internet's self-appointed Che Guevaras and vigilante groups, you are not likely to be bothered by hackers of the moralistic, anarchistic or art-for-art's-sake types. These greatly outnumber the others and are usually much better equipped to hack into your systems than the occasional, though highly newsworthy, Net-based extortionist.

➡ HACKING IN PERSPECTIVE

Anti-hacking security measures are always a matter of degree. If you have something very important to protect, you will spend the money and put in the multi-level firewalls and other devices that may be needed to keep determined and sophisticated hackers out. Barclays Bank, for example, an obvious target for mischief, has three major firewalls in place and spends nearly £1.5 million a year just to maintain them and keep them shipshape. If you are not such a high-risk target, layers of encryption, frequently changed passwords and the electronic passports known as 'digital certificates' are the sort of tools you would use to build up your defences. Depressingly enough, experience in Britain and the USA has shown that serious hacking is more often an inside job than the work of outside assailants – grudges are a more common motive than greed. Digital certificates are particularly helpful against the enemy within, as a deterrent as well as an obstacle, because they make it starkly clear that any suspicious activity will be traced straight back to a single authorised user.

In the end, as various security breaches at the Pentagon have shown, watertight, 100-per-cent-hackproof security is virtually impossible. In practice, though, it's unnecessary. If you heap up your defences high enough, the effort needed to penetrate them – in terms of cash, computing power, time and so on – can be made so great that the ordinary criminal can't afford the resources to tackle a project where success is far from guaranteed. In this respect, the professionals are less of a threat than the dedicated amateurs, the hackers who are driven by the idea of a challenge or a crusade, rather than the profit motive.

➡ DON'T PANIC

If half the last decade's scare stories about the dangers of hacking were well founded, the Internet could not possibly have developed as it has, though there's always room for one more lurid rumour. Talk of a new virus that would allow hackers to take over your PC, stop and start it at will and run it by remote control came to a head when a sinister program called Back Orifice (in a jibing pun at Microsoft's Back Office software) was unveiled in August 1998. But while hackers claimed it would unleash an epidemic, Microsoft emphasised that accessing the Net through a properly constructed firewall should guarantee companies complete safety. And because the new virus is delivered as an e-mail attachment, those without firewalls can also ensure no harm is done by regularly updating their virus-checkers and refusing to open unexpected e-mail attachments without scanning them first.

Unnerving though this new virus may sound, there is apparently less to it than meets the eye. Within days of its launch, the experts of Symantec's Norton AntiVirus team were delivering a reassuring verdict. It cannot attack PCs using Windows NT or the old Windows 3.x operating systems, they announced, nor those connected to the Net via service providers using 'dynamic IP assignment' – which covers virtually all home and very small business users – nor those protected by firewalls, which covers most corporate users.

The threat to unprotected machines running Windows 98 and Windows 95 is real enough to warrant extra care and a general ban within any company on downloading programs and e-mail attachments from unknown sources. But Symantec and the other industry leaders were confidently offering free online updates to combat BO less than a week after it hit the headlines. However ingenious and persistent the hacking community may be, there are a lot of very bright people and the vested interests of the whole commercial world ranged against them. It may be a running battle between the hackers and virus creators and the Men in Black with their mission to keep our planet safe for democracy and business, but the great weight of resources will always favour the bugbusters.

Appendix B
Seven ways to make a fortune via the Internet

Here they are, as promised in Chapter 1. Here are our seven ideas that you can adopt or exploit to make a fortune via the Internet, all viable and none of them half as crazy as some of the megalomaniac visions that have successfully found venture capital backing in the USA in the last couple of years. The really smart way, of course, was to be there right at the beginning, start a company doing something (at times, it seemed, almost anything) to do with the Web and then sell out for several million dollars, after creating a stir but no profits. There are examples too numerous – and too libellous – to mention, but that particular bout of tulipomania has passed. We are going to have to work for our spoils now, and here are some of the most promising ways to go about it, each of them tapping into the particular strengths and characteristics of the Internet and the World Wide Web.

1. *http://www.ourtownclassifieds.co.uk* – Local newspapers have been really slow on the uptake. Make sure you cut across their catchment areas, so your local ad would have to be in two or more papers to cover the same area. The Web may be a global medium, but it's also brilliant for very localised classified advertising. No printing, no distribution, no waiting for Thursday morning (you update daily or even more often, and that means punters come to you several times a week). Charge for cars and houses, make all other private ads free and take display advertising from local companies.

2. *http://www.j-watch.co.uk* – Instant glimpse of traffic conditions on M25, M42 or the black spot near you, from a roof-mounted vidcam on a house or factory. J14 on the M25, just by Heathrow, would be a good place to start. Build a chain, with hotlinks from each junction site to the next, of course. Revenue comes from advertising now, plus automated micropayments of a couple of pence per view once that technology is available. Eventually, glancing at your sites becomes pure daily habit for car-borne commuters – and hourly routine for courier and transport firms.

3. *http://www.3legssoftware.com* – As described in Chapter 1, make accelerated development (six months' work in eight or nine weeks) your USP and go for winning big, high-margin bids. If you can't run offices of your own in the world's other two shift-zones, form tight alliances with people on the ground in America and Asia or Australia whose skills match yours. The same opportunities apply in engineering and electrical design, publishing, architecture, drug research – wherever being first to market has major payoffs. Not impossible without an intranet, e-mail and Internet-based videoconferencing to tie everyone's work together and ensure smooth baton changes, just fraught with dangers the new technology can overcome.

4. *http://www.minorsoccertv.co.uk* – First you provide proper, informed soccer coverage of everything from the Conference down, including all those teams you only hear about when the FA Cup first round throws up a giant-killer or two. Then you introduce live coverage of … well, the best standard games that are free and affordable to show. This TV station isn't broadcasting, because no signal goes out; people simply connect to view your Website. The Webcam technology is relatively cheap – very good equipment would still be under £10,000 and you could start off with a lot less. The point is, though, that it's not just football. There are big, but fragmented, markets out there for squash, tennis, league cricket, ladies' bowls, minor-league rugby, stock car racing, go-karting, gliding, surfing and countless other competitive and non-competitive sports. This whole area is going to be huge. Password-protected subscription would probably be the first

payment method, moving to pay-per-view micropayments when that becomes possible.

5. *http://www.sitetrades.co.uk* – Remember when the only people who had mobiles were City whizz-kids and builders? The building trades have always been quick to catch on, but only when they can see a direct use for new technology. Here's one. Casual day-rate site labourers get good money, but it's a hit-and-miss business finding the sites that need people. A continuously updated Web-based clearing house could stop people having to travel to sites where there may be no work. Day-rate chippies, plasterers, painters, snaggers and electricians could also see, at a glance, where the work was. Don't charge the people – get the building companies to subscribe. The lads will soon work out that the kit they need to access the Web is paid for in three or four days.

6. *http://www.keepitalive.co.uk* – Stocking and finding service for repair parts for out-of-date domestic equipment and appliances, stretching back over the decades. Serves both trade and general public, with credit card ordering through online forms. Like Amazon.com and Dell, though, you've got to work hard at getting the post-order fulfilment right to make it work.

7. *http://www.nichepaper.com* – Find a tightly defined superniche and make it your own, delivering instantly to a scattered worldwide audience of subscribers by e-mail. Investment matters are the easiest area, since people understand that a single nugget of information can put them on to an idea that pays for your newsletter for years. No niche is too tight, though – try Indonesian Telecoms Investor or Government Surplus Vehicles Worldwide.

Good luck. Let us know how you get on, via our Websites (*http:// members.aol.com/shircore* or *http://www.lime-media.com*) or e-mail (*shircorebk@aol.com* or *richard.lander@lime-media.com*), and do pass on any interesting case histories that might be enlightening and usable in the next edition of *Mastering the Internet*. Above all, remember that, extraordinary though the new technologies of the Internet may be, it is what you can imagine doing with them that will make the difference. We're standing here with a new world at our feet and the last thing we need is voices from behind saying 'That's not how it has to be done.' So dream it, think it through and do it – and see what happens. There is more opportunity to upset old monopolies, shatter established patterns and create new structures and companies now than at any time for 50 years. Let's see what we can make of it all.

ABOUT THE AUTHORS

Ian Shircore is an author, management coach and marketing consultant. His work is concerned with the forces acting to change the shape of business – including technologies such as the World Wide Web and the new emphasis on systematic approaches to the 'soft skills' of management. He draws on twenty years' experience in big-company consultancy projects, writing speeches for BT's directors, editing staff and customer newspapers and advising on communications issues of all kinds. His clients include institutions such as the Treasury, London Business School and the Law Society and businesses ranging from Sony, Diageo, ICL to the International Herald Tribune. As a trainer, he teaches a range of communication and management skills, leading small-group courses for clients including BT, Ashridge Management College, the TECs and the Human Capital training group.

Other books:
Treasure Hunting, Macdonald, (1980)
Right for Your Reader. A Painless Style Guide for Managers, BT, (1994)
Smart Office: 11 Steps to the User-Friendly Office (with Judith Verity), Bloomsbury, (1996)
NLP and the New Manager (with Ian McDermott), Orion Business, (1998)

Richard Lander is an author, journalist and consultant to businesses in the areas of media relations, business strategy and Internet use. After working as a full-time business journalist for more than a decade with national and international leaders such as Reuters, *The Independent* and *The Times*, he took an MBA at City University Business School before establishing his own London-based consultancy, Lime Media. His firm's blue chip clients have included the NCR Corporation, BT, Dow Jones and Edelman Worldwide Public Relations. He contributed the key chapter on Internet commerce for *The Icon Critical Dictionary of Global Economics*, Icon Books, (1999)

Index